HEALING IS THE NEW HIGH

HEALING IS THE NEW HIGH

A GUIDE TO OVERCOMING EMOTIONAL TURMOIL AND FINDING FREEDOM

VEX KING

HAY HOUSE

HAY HOUSE INDIA
New Delhi • London • Sydney
Carlsbad, California • New York City

Hay House Publishers (India) Pvt Ltd
Muskaan Complex, Plot No. 3, B-2, Vasant Kunj, New Delhi – 110070, India

Hay House LLC, P.O. Box 5100, Carlsbad, CA 92018-5100, USA
Hay House UK Ltd, 1st Floor, Crawford Corner, 91-93 Baker Street, London W1U 6QQ, UK
Hay House Australia Publishing Pty Ltd, 18/36 Ralph St., Alexandria NSW 2015, Australia

Email: contact@hayhouse.co.in
Website: www.hayhouse.co.in

The information given in this book should not be treated as a substitute for professional medical advice; always consult a medical practitioner. Any use of information in this book is at the reader's discretion and risk. Neither the author nor the publisher can be held responsible for any loss, claim or damage arising out of the use, or misuse, of the suggestions made, the failure to take medical advice or for any material on third-party websites.

First published by Hay House India, 2021
Reprint, 2025
18 17 16 15 14 13 12 11 10 9

ISBN 978-93-88302-69-2

Printed at Thomson Press Ltd

FSC www.fsc.org
MIX
Paper | Supporting responsible forestry
FSC® C010615

Hay House is committed to a sustainable future for our business, our readers and our planet. This book is made from Forest Stewardship Council® certified paper.

In memory of my nan, Tara,

who I lost in the process of writing this book.

Contents

Foreword

We live in a world in need of more heroes, wisdom and love.

Amid the tectonic change, relentless disruption and new ways of being, it becomes so easy to wish for lights and luminaries to show up who will guide us forward. Through the good times and the unfortunate. Into the beauty of a better future.

And yet—there is no doubt—that you are the wayshower that you seek.

...You have the strength, insight and bravery to handcraft the life you deserve.

...You have the potential to make your promise real and the gorgeous ability to push your stardust into society.

...You have the mental toughness and spiritual genius needed to help make our little planet a better place to inhabit.

And you have what it takes to truly be an inspirational force to everyone that you meet. So people leave you bigger than you found them.

When Vex asked me to write the foreword to this book, I was delighted to say yes. Because he gets it.

He gets that the only real guru resides within yourself.

And that everyday people are the truest of all heroes.

And that for our world to grow better, each of us must stop excusing and do the work required to make our selves better. And stronger. And wiser. And immensely more caring.

So, I pray that you savor this book. Read it with an open mind and with a careful heart. Consume the lines slowly, intentionally and embrace the offering in ways that allow them to touch your center.

So that when you're done, you walk out into the world. Born anew.

Robin Sharma

Author of the #1 worldwide bestsellers
The Monk Who Sold His Ferrari and *The 5AM Club*

Why does this book exist?

This book has been a long time coming. I've written it (at last) because my life hasn't always been easy and because I know that *your* life hasn't always been easy. I've written it because through developing and using the inner healing techniques I share in these pages, I've been able to let go of my troubled past and heal my emotional pain, or trauma. I've also helped others move forward on their own healing journey.

You don't need a guru to do inner healing work. Nor do you need to spend a huge amount of money on courses, or quit your job and find hours and hours each day to practice it. You can heal from your trauma and other emotional wounds in a long-lasting way by using the practical exercises in this book. Simple, accessible, and with the power to produce exceptional results, they're underpinned by the principle of raising your *vibration* (this is the energy that courses through you and that you radiate out into the world around you).

If you've read my first book, *Good Vibes, Good Life*, you'll know that vibrating on a higher level can help you manifest great things and change your life. In this book I'll show you how you can become your own healer to raise your vibration.

That's not to say that your healing journey can't be hindered, or that results will always be immediate and clear. One of the biggest obstacles to inner healing work is a desire to cling on to the past – our inability to let go of what's *been* prevents us from moving forward into what *could* be. That's why the first chapters of this book focus on developing our ability to let go. And then we step into the present, before looking to the future.

Inner healing is the act of letting go of past conditioning, creating a new, empowering belief system for ourselves, and embracing the unknowns of the future with the confidence that we're strong and capable – no matter what comes our way. You'll come to realize that you have the ability to move forward with confidence, and with a steady belief in your own resilience and strength.

Trauma is the enduring emotional and psychological pain that often results when we live through an experience that our brain is unable to process properly for some reason. Sometimes, that lack of effective processing occurs because the experience was deeply disturbing, shocking, upsetting, frightening, or hard to understand, or because it happened to us when we were very young and our brain hadn't developed sufficiently to work through it fully. But trauma can be more subtle, too – experiences that confuse us, or that make us feel ashamed or humiliated, can settle into us as deep emotional wounds, even though no one else notices them.

Here's the thing about trauma: we've all suffered it in some form or other, but almost none of us were taught from a young age how to handle it. As a result, a vast number of people turn to a method of self-medication to manage their pain, whether they're struggling emotionally, physically, or spiritually.

Certain highs, produced by taking synthetic or natural drugs, or alcohol, or feeding an addiction to food, sex, work, or social media (to name but a few), make us *feel* as though we've transcended our struggles. But that feeling is temporary. At best, it leaves us needing more of that high just to get through the days; and at worst, the high is followed by a low that's deep, dark, and may feel intensely desperate.

So, I'm striving to let go of false highs, however they show up in my life, and instead to access a more truthful, sustainable, and less tumultuous high: the high of genuine inner healing. This doesn't disappear and leave you feeling empty and lost. It builds, and it builds *you*, until you see everything with new clarity.

This is the high that I'm writing about and sharing with my clients every day. And I believe that now is the perfect time to focus on it – because we're living through a shift in human consciousness, and we're all increasingly driven to change the way we interact with ourselves, with others, and with the world around us.

You, like every other person reading this book, are playing an active role in embracing this shift. You're part of something special: a move toward living better and caring more.

I'm not a doctor or a psychologist, and this book is not a substitute for medical advice or the help of a professional therapist. I'm someone who's learnt from my experiences, mistakes, and growth, and created a life filled with happiness, love, and hope. As a mind coach, I've successfully helped hundreds of thousands of people, both online and offline – from celebrities and business owners to people who thought that happiness and success simply wouldn't happen for them – to exercise new and powerful ways of thinking that bring about beautiful and positive changes to transform their lives.

Inner healing is the act of letting go of past conditioning, creating a new, empowering belief system for ourselves, and embracing the unknowns of the future with the confidence that we're strong and capable – no matter what comes our way.

And this book is intended to give you the tools you need to do the same. If you're working through therapy at the moment, or would like to soon, this book can be a supportive addition to that process.

Inner healing is a means for creating a better world, and so we must *invest* in it – not only for our own sake but also for that of others. As the popular saying goes, 'hurt people hurt people.' And in contrast, I firmly believe that healed people *help* people. Which is why it's my honor to help you heal.

Post pictures or your favorite images,
pages, quotes, and experiences related
to this book on social media using

#HealingIsTheNewHigh

so I can see them and share them on my page.

Introduction

We'd had an argument. I can't remember what it was about, but it was a big one. I had a funny feeling that night – unsettled, as if something big was going to happen. It could have been due to the argument, or discomfort rooted in paranoia – I knew she was heading out to a bar, and she always got plenty of attention.

On top of that, she hadn't texted me. I'd always get a text goodnight, even if we'd fallen out, but that night I got nothing. My mind was crowded – too many conflicting thoughts were blaring out – and I just couldn't sleep:

Maybe I've taken things too far.

Maybe something's happened to her.

I think I need to text her. No, wait – she was wrong, not me.

What if she's moved on already and she's with someone else?

No, she won't be – that's deceitful, and I know her. I can trust her because she loves me with all her heart. After all, she's the one who pursued me when I wasn't interested.

Finally, I plucked up the courage to text her goodnight.

She sent her response in the early hours of the morning. She poured her heart out to me, saying she loved me and wanted to patch things up. Apparently, her life wouldn't be the same without me.

I bought the idea, I really did.

But then a friend sent me a text, and in an instant, even before I'd opened it, I felt anxious. I just had a *bad* feeling. And I was right. The text said that my girlfriend had gone home with his cousin.

I felt angry and disappointed, but also doubtful. This particular friend didn't like the idea of the two of us and he had his reasons. Maybe he was trying to put me off her. But then, why would he lie? After all, the guy he was accusing of being with my girlfriend was his cousin. Also, my friend had existed in my world long before my girlfriend had, so I should have been able to trust him before I trusted her.

And to be honest, I owed it to him to believe him because I'd broken the 'Bro Code' by getting together with my girlfriend despite knowing he'd had history with her. Our love story was flawed to begin with and it should never have existed.

Eventually, I confronted her. And she was appalled. She denied it and told me my friend was jealous and trying to get between us. She made me feel bad for believing him and not trusting her. She seemed open and vulnerable, and told me she was deeply hurt. I felt guilty – she was that convincing.

And here was my problem. Every time we argued, a new story would emerge and the narrative would be the same. She was unfaithful to me on multiple occasions, and each time, she'd buy her way back into my life and emotionally manipulate me into believing her faults were my flaws.

This pattern was becoming embarrassing for me. I had a reputation as the boy who got the girl – not, perhaps, because I was good-looking but because I had a charming nature, was popular with my friends, and had a good heart. Now, I was becoming known as the boy with the girlfriend every other boy was hooking up with.

My closest friends had warned me; even strangers had. They told me to use her for what she was good for: physical intimacy. But I was in way too deep, and I didn't believe in being in a relationship if there was no future in it. I didn't want to hurt her. And I saw light within her that no one else could see.

People labeled me 'whipped' and 'sprung,' and eventually I responded to that by pretending to use my girlfriend for sexual encounters. But this was a lie. I felt as if I needed her. It was painful with her, but my life would seem more painful without her. The pain wasn't just emotional, either: I was getting into fights with other men over her. Men who teased me about what they were doing with her, and how I wasn't good enough for her because her attention was swaying toward them.

I'd always heard that it's guys who are the players, the scumbags, the ones who have all the control. But I'd lost mine. Here I was, a hopeless romantic foolishly believing in an illusion I'd shaped from my own imagination about this other person, and the connection I thought I could have with her.

As time went on and new evidence came to light, I finally hit boiling point. I knew I couldn't be with her, and that I had to remove myself from this relationship and not buy into her words and emotional manipulation.

I decided to put on a front. I told her that if we were to move forward with our relationship, she'd have to admit to everything she'd done. Deep down, I knew that nothing she could say would be enough because I'd already decided to move on, regardless of how uncomfortable it would be. But she didn't know this.

And her response really did put this into perspective. I wasn't even shocked as she told me about all the times she'd betrayed me – I'd always known it was true, but I'd just refused to accept it. I almost needed the words to come out of her mouth. What was increasingly painful at that point was the blame she put on me. In no way was I perfect, but she made me out to be a failure and created doubt in me, even though I'd been faithful and loving throughout our relationship. The only times I'd really given her a reason to look elsewhere was when we'd argued over my accusations of her cheating.

Afterward, it was so hard not to text her at night, like I always had. We'd had several breakups before this final one, and I'd always reopened our communication to get closure. However, what I was really doing was keeping my routine with her alive. I was reentering my comfort zone by speaking to her, even if it was just to argue.

So I had to exercise huge willpower to stop myself from responding to her text messages, which said things like:

'If you truly cared about me, you'd reply.'

'If you loved me at all, you'd want to work this out.'

'I miss you and will do anything to be with you.'

Nevertheless, this really was the final straw. The heartache was too great this time, and I was willing to undergo the pain of change in order to break my attachment to her. I had to resist the urge. I had to start a new chapter.

Although I didn't know it at the time, in the months following the breakup I went through a traumatic grief reaction and experienced a number of intense thoughts, physical sensations, and emotions. With traumatic loss it's really hard for the mind to wrap itself around the concept that this thing's really happened and that it's true. Below, I've described my symptoms and their trajectory:

Denial I was still a little unsure if this really was the end. I questioned whether or not we should actually try to make things work. I mean, if this was love, we shouldn't just give up on it.

Hatred Hate is a strong word and I don't like using it, but this is how I'd describe what I felt toward her. She'd embarrassed me, played me for a fool, and got in the way of my most important friendships. But I wasn't just angry with *her* – I felt anger toward a whole gender: women. I felt they couldn't be trusted, and that nice guys do indeed finish last.

Disappointment I went into a deep mode of overthinking – questioning why things hadn't worked out in the way I thought they should have. *What had gone wrong? Why had she done it? She'd said she loved me!*

And when she stopped sending me text messages – to which she was getting no response – I even said to myself: *If she really loved me, why would she let this end?*

Self-blame I went through a period where I blamed myself for the breakup. *Maybe if I'd paid more attention to her, she wouldn't have shifted her attention elsewhere*, I thought. I'd recall statements that she'd made, in order to evoke guilt in myself. I even began questioning my looks and my physical attributes, which just left me feeling even more insecure.

Anti-love I told myself I'd never love again and that I'd never commit to anyone. I actually convinced myself that I needed to become more of a player. Although this role wasn't in my nature, and I never quite fulfilled it, I did start to have more random hook-ups. But I often felt ashamed and disappointed in myself after them.

Moving through the pain toward healing

After the end of that relationship, I kept telling myself not to get too deep with people. I had a guard up, and as soon as I sensed I was falling for a girl or I felt threatened by one (as if she were going to hurt me), I tried to hurt her first and broke things off without giving her a chance. I had trust issues and I never admitted to them. If a girl had a close male friend, I'd assume the worst, and this created problems in my romantic relationships.

This often meant I wouldn't give girls the treatment they deserved, or that I was capable of. And although I believe that everything happens for a reason and things have worked out as they were meant to, I'm truly sorry that I inflicted my own pain and insecurities onto my romantic partners. I was always the one to end these relationships, but I take responsibility for the times when I didn't act with love, compassion, and understanding.

The truth is, after that breakup, I needed to undergo a whole healing process. The relationship had severely dented my belief in others and, more importantly, in myself. The flaws in my perception meant I could never love with all of my being. I was unable to turn up in a relationship with genuine love to give – I was always trying to receive love, and the moment I felt it wasn't being delivered in the way I wanted it to be, I'd switch off.

What I didn't know was that I was already healing. From the moment I made the difficult decision to end that relationship for good, every minute, every painful emotion, and every flicker of rage or doubt became vital to my ability to become the person I am today. The person I so badly wanted to be.

I'm not saying that I'm 'done' – there's always work to do and there'll always be wounds to acknowledge and heal. But when I started to take an active role in my own healing, I realized I'd started the work years earlier. I just hadn't known how to understand it, or how to interpret the moments of clarity I experienced, or how to *use* my emotions to propel me forward instead of becoming stuck in a hole.

Even in the early stages of my relationship with my wife, I acted on the pain of my past. Fortunately, my wife had the capacity – and the willingness – to hold space for me to heal in. It was my responsibility to commit to my healing journey, and also to hold space for hers, which she was equally devoted to. We were both grieving over past relationships. And although it took time, when I learnt to put my ego aside and welcome the potential of a new life, there was no going back.

Your journey toward healing

This isn't a book about relationships. Well, it is in a way, because relationships (not necessarily romantic ones) are always an important element of a person's healing journey. But I want to make it clear that I'm not sharing the story of this breakup with you because this book is about breakups. Instead, I'm sharing it to lay bare a little part of myself – to reveal a pain that I've felt, and healed from, in all its ugliness.

This story also reveals some of the things about myself that I've been most ashamed of over the years – paranoia, jealousy, ego, insecurity, and a willingness to believe lies because I didn't want to be alone. Being ready to reveal those darker parts of ourselves is vital if we want to draw light into our life again. And if I'm going to ask *you* to do it, you have to know that I'm willing to do it too.

My intention in this book is to give you the support and motivation necessary for you to embark on your personal journey to inner healing. I understand that some journeys will be harder than others. You might be healing from a relationship breakup, sure, but if you're healing from something else, you're welcome here too. If you've been through a traumatic experience that you still struggle to speak about, you're welcome here. And whether you're recommitting yourself to healing old emotional wounds or battling with something new and raw, you're welcome here.

You'll gain insight into your own lived experience, and discover opportunities to reflect on and see your pain in a new way. I won't pretend that every page will be easy to read, or that every moment of this journey will feel *good* to you – because the reality of inner healing is that it hurts. You have to face up to experiences and emotions that you've tried to squash, feelings that you've hidden away in the recesses of your mind.

You have to confront your own perspective on the world, on yourself, and on other people. And you must invite yourself to accept the possibility that you were wrong – that things weren't always the way you thought they were.

One thing I know about trauma is that it distorts and intensifies every negative thought, feeling, physical sensation and so on that we have. Trauma is like being covered with open wounds and wading into the ocean. A person who is whole and healed will very likely experience a positive sensation, especially if the water's warm and inviting and they love the ocean; however, someone who's experiencing trauma will immediately feel pain as the saltwater burns each wound. Trauma makes us thin-skinned, overly sensitive, hypervigilant, and prone to pain. And it's often all-encompassing, too, so our attention is focused on the pain and on desperately trying to avoid more of it.

When you experience the world through the lens of trauma, it's easy to miss the opportunity for positive experiences. Healing isn't a linear process – we move two steps forward and one step back on all levels. Gradually, healing can ripple out, like a stone tossed into a pool of still water; each ripple penetrates the trauma and replaces it with healing energy. Committing to the practices of healing is the first step. Be patient with yourself, get support where you can, and positive changes will occur without you even noticing.

No matter how skeptical or unsure you feel right now, you're here – reading these words and taking the first steps on your journey to powerful inner healing. You're doing it already, and with this book in your hands, you don't have to do it alone. Every chapter includes the gift of one or two practical exercises that will gradually lead you to a new sense of confidence and freedom. Each exercise is simple, and you'll learn how to integrate it into your daily life in a way that makes your healing process a part of your everyday.

Inner healing isn't something you do in the evenings or on weekends – you'll learn to work on it all the time. And I'll share more of myself along the way, of course; I'll tell you about the experiences that have helped me and that I hope will remind you that you're in good company.

One thing I know about trauma is that it distorts and intensifies every negative thought, feeling, and physical sensation we have. Trauma makes us thin-skinned, overly sensitive, hypervigilant, and prone to pain. And it's often all-encompassing, so our attention is focused on the pain and on desperately trying to avoid it.

If your attention is fading here, I'd like you to ask yourself why. Is there a voice inside your head saying, *This isn't for me – other people can heal, but I can't?* That voice is your pain talking – and it's wrong. Because here's the thing: inner healing isn't something that only 'healers' or 'spiritual people' can do. Every person is their own healer. *You're* your own healer – you have all of the tools for growth and change already within you, and this book will teach you how to use them.

You'll discover how to explore the edges of your experience with curiosity, not fear. And ask yourself questions that will begin to take down the walls you've built to protect yourself from being hurt, allowing you to walk with new ease through life.

Questions like...

- Why do I respond like that?
- Why is that particular memory so important to me?
- Why do I base my assumptions about the world on that memory, and not this other one?
- Who do I trust? Who *can* I trust?

- What would happen if I told someone this?
- How would I choose to live if I felt completely free?

So, come with me. I welcome you on this journey. And perhaps, soon, you'll be able to welcome *yourself* on the journey to true peace, every single day.

CHAPTER 1

How many bodies?

Working through each layer of the self is the key to inner healing.

Before we get into the depths of inner healing work, I want to take a moment – in fact, a short chapter – to explain why the book is structured in the way it is, and how that structure will support you on your journey. The order of the chapters is no accident, and it's important that you know there's a reason for *every page* – even when you're working through those that you find hard or challenging; and even when you're working through those that feel easy and comfortable.

As I've already hinted, I wasn't always down with the idea of 'healing,' and definitely not with notions of spirituality or internal growth. I was focused on other things: being a man (or more specifically, living in a way that I perceived was 'manly'), achieving tangible goals, and getting the material stuff that I thought would make my life feel valuable and good. Because of this, I totally relate to people who are turned off by 'growth' language, or who think that spiritual practices are just not for them.

Does that sound like you? If so, I'll tell you this now – you won't be expected to suspend your disbelief as you read this book. I'll ask you to go into it with an open mind and a willingness to play around with concepts you may not have considered before, but I won't tell you that you have to become a spiritual person or start believing in magic or crystals in order to feel better and open yourself up to more positivity and freedom.

That said, while I was planning this work, I *really* wanted to weave into it some of the principles of yoga philosophy because these have guided me so brilliantly on my own journey. Many people get into the physical practice of yoga and then discover yoga philosophy later, but I got into the philosophy *first* – I was inspired by the vast number of people who credit their yoga practice with some form of healing or growth or life improvement.

So one day, I bought a copy of a book called *The Yoga Sutras of Patanjali*. The word 'sutra' roughly translates from Sanskrit to English as 'thread,' and this book is an exploration of the threads of knowledge, or teachings, that make up the holistic practice of yoga. As well as containing English translations of the sutras, it also offers guidance on how each one can help lead the yoga practitioner toward their true Self – toward enlightenment.

I do a little physical yoga practice now too, but my focus is still on meditation – a practice in which an individual is fully immersed in the present moment through their senses, while observing calmly and without judgment their thoughts, emotions, and bodily sensations. Nevertheless, the *Yoga Sutras* have become my Holy Grail.

I'm not convinced that 'enlightenment' is the only worthy goal in life. The idea that we are all we need and that we can be free from desire and blissfully happy and peaceful every second of every day for the rest of our lives *sounds* great, sure. However, I don't believe that our sole purpose on this Earth is to reject all the day-to-day stuff and rise above the need for connection with other humans, or personal comforts, or desire, and be pure and perfect beings.

To be honest, I've often questioned whether this is even possible, especially given that, over the years, many of the people who've claimed to be enlightened have turned out to be cult leader-like figures. If someone hurt or abused another person through their own desire or because they were affected by the power they attained as others started to believe they were enlightened... Well, they couldn't really have been enlightened, right?

Personally, I've met only a handful of people who I believe come close to the idea of enlightenment as it's described in many ancient texts, and even they have their limitations. But when I started reading *The Yoga Sutras of Patanjali*, I realized that I could benefit from it hugely without having to believe in that specific outcome.

Although the book is full of detailed direction on how best to live our daily life, its approach to this is surprisingly undogmatic. I found that what I got from it, ultimately, was a kind of confidence that I could feel *free*; that I could be liberated. Not in the traditional sense of enlightenment, but in the sense that I could be liberated from the things about me that stopped me from being confident, secure, and excited about my future.

I could take what I needed from the book and its wisdom and put those teachings into my daily life in a way that worked for me, and felt real and genuinely helpful, rather than fluffy or fake or pretentious. I could use the lessons in the book in a practical way, and pass over the parts that felt completely irrelevant to me.

Like the bit that says that your yoga practice space should 'have a small door, and no window; it should be free from holes, cavities, inequalities, high steps, and low descents. It should be smeared with cow-dung, not infested by vermin, with a terrace in front, a good well, and the whole surrounded by a wall."[1]

Yeah. Not every word in that book makes sense to a reader living in a developed country in the 21st century. And that's OK – it doesn't mean that nothing valuable can be gained from reading the text. Honest. And I did gain a lot of valuable insight from it.

A light went on

As I read *The Yoga Sutras of Patanjali,* something happened: I began to let go of the things that hurt me. I began to accept that I didn't have to be so affected by other people's actions. I found that I could choose who I was, and most importantly, that who I was didn't have to be changed by what other people thought of me.

I gained a new kind of steadiness, and that steadiness has been the anchor that's kept me strong as I've moved through the process of healing, and more letting go, and of shedding beliefs and impressions from my past and becoming who I really want to be.

So, when I knew I was going to write this book, I struggled with an internal conflict. Although I wanted to include some of the

1 Sri Swami Satchidananda, 2012. *The Yoga Sutras of Patanjali*. Integral Yoga Publications, p.110.

principles of yoga philosophy – the things that'd helped me so much – I also wanted, even more, to write a book that *wasn't* full of Sanskrit or fluffy stuff that I knew would put readers off. Because a few years ago, *I* would have been put off by all that stuff, and as a result, I'd have missed out on the opportunity to improve my life, and to build a better relationship with my past and with my current self.

I didn't want anyone – maybe *you* – to reject the idea of inner healing because it was packed in with loads of spiritual jargon. None of the concepts from yogic texts would mean anything to you unless you'd already experienced them in a practical way in your own life. But I knew that if there was a way for me to enable you to *experience* them and to make them part of your healing process, without just talking about them endlessly, they *would* help you. I knew that they'd add a lot to your life, and to your wellbeing, and to your capacity for feeling better.

I decided to talk to my friend Isla, a yoga teacher and fellow mind coach. I laid out my predicament: 'I don't want to leave all this stuff out. You know how much it could add... I feel like I'd be letting readers down if I didn't find a way to put these concepts in the book. But I don't want to push people away. I don't want it to be another book about healing through yoga that only people who already do yoga will read.'

'OK,' Isla said, 'so you want to give them the experience of *using* these principles and *feeling* them, without telling them to chant Sanskrit or asking them to stop being themselves?'

'Right.'

'So, could the book *itself* be the experience? Do you really have to talk about those concepts the whole way through? When you're actually physically practicing yoga, it's not this academic thing. You're not thinking about philosophy all the time – you're just doing it, and the benefits come from just doing it. Is there a way the book could be a way of just *doing* it?'

That was it. I needed to make the book an *experience* – not simply a text to read, but a journey through the self. And then it hit me – the book's structure had to form the foundations of that journey. So I scoured the books on my shelves and beyond for clues and filled notebooks with ideas, looking for the perfect healing structure hidden in reams and centuries of knowledge and philosophy.

A journey through the self

In *The Yoga Sutras of Patanjali* we learn about the five 'bodies,' or layers, that make up our whole self. This is the most common teaching about the bodies, but it's not the only one. I began structuring this book with the 'five bodies' in mind, but it didn't quite click; I found I needed more space – more layers to move through in order to deepen this inner healing work. So I turned to a different interpretation of the bodies, one that's used in some schools of yoga, including Kundalini:

We have seven bodies.

Er... what? OK, stay with me. Like I said, this book isn't going to be full of spiritual jargon, but I do need to include a few words about this concept here, for the reasons I mentioned earlier. So that you know there's a purpose to every page. Even the ones you'd rather skip.

Instead of taking the ideas that follow literally, take them as a way of thinking about the 'self' differently, or more holistically. Because in our modern world we tend to simplify the idea of the whole human – and that means we're not very good at working with all our complexities, and different layers, and the subtle parts of ourselves that affect every experience, feeling, and thought we have.

According to ancient texts and teachings, each of us has a physical body and a number of 'subtle' bodies. In the particular interpretation I'm working with here, there are seven bodies.[2] The globally known Indian guru Osho is perhaps the person best known for talking about, working with, and teaching the seven bodies concept, and he argues that only when we acknowledge and care for each of the bodies equally will we be peaceful, creative, and complete.[3]

The physical body is just one expression of us, the most obvious one. But all seven bodies need to be healthy and cared for in order for our whole self to feel vibrant.[4] To vibrate on a high level and feel alive and rich with energy and positivity, each one of our seven bodies, or layers of the self, needs to be working in harmony with the others.

Energy isn't an imaginary spiritual concept – it's a reality of our existence. A recent report on Energy Medicine in the journal *Global Advances in Health and Medicine* found that energetic therapies – including those based on energetic technologies and those that

---

2 Isaac, S. and Newhouse, F. (2001), *The Seven Bodies Unveiled*. Bluestar Communications Corporation.

3 Osho (1996), *In Search of the Miraculous: Chakras, Kundalini and the Seven Bodies*. C.W. Daniel Co. Ltd.

4 Little, T. (2016), *Yoga of the Subtle Body: A Guide to the Physical and Energetic Anatomy of Yoga*. Shambhala Publications Inc.

use direct human touch – are often merged with biochemistry techniques, and this blend of therapy and cutting-edge science could bring about great advances in the way medical professionals are able to treat physical, mental, and emotional disorders.[5]

Because where modern medicine, including mental health treatment, fails is in its scope – it doesn't look at the whole person, the whole being, the whole body, the whole self. We're not machines. We can't erase trauma by getting rid of its symptoms. We have to go deeper – into the subtle energies that are always at work within us.

But this book isn't *about* the seven bodies. Instead, it's an experiential journey *through* them. It uses the seven bodies not as empirical fact but as a powerful language of understanding – a framework to move through the healing process in a way that builds and takes *all* aspects of our being into account, without neglecting those areas of ourselves that we often ignore when we try to fix only the surface wounds that are easy to see.

5 Ross, C.L. (2019), 'Energy Medicine: Current Status and Future Perspectives': www.ncbi.nlm.nih.gov/pmc/articles/PMC6396053 [Accessed January 2, 2021]

To vibrate on a high level and feel alive and rich with energy and positivity, each one of our seven bodies, or layers of the self, needs to be working in harmony with the others.

Our seven bodies

This book is a kind of meditation in itself; it's a practical journey, a lived exploration. Right now, I'm going to lay out the seven bodies with a very, very brief description of each one, so you understand how we'll work through the layers of the self as we go on through these pages.

And after that? We'll just do it.

The physical body

This one doesn't need much explanation – we all know our physical body. Usually, it's the only body we perceive. It's the interpreter between the self and the world; we use it to experience, to sense, to feel, and to express.

The etheric body

This body is closely linked with our emotions. It's said to develop between the ages of seven and 14, but it can continue to change throughout our lives if we work closely with it. This body is where we store our emotional experiences, which then go on to form our perception of ourselves, other people, and the world.

The astral body

The astral body is associated with reason, intellect, and logical thinking. It develops through our interactions with the world – so, the way that we use logic and reason, and thinking power, depends a lot on how and where we grow up. However, like all of the bodies, the astral body can develop, and we can focus on it to change the way we think, and to create new patterns, habits, and new motivation to learn and change.

The mental body

The mental body goes a step beyond the astral body; instead of logic and reason, it's all about intuition and deeper mental power. This doesn't have to be esoteric. We all have intuition; we all have the capacity to sense things, and to predict things, and to pick up on tiny signals to build a picture. The mental body creates a more subjective world, but that world is as important as any objective experience (if there is such a thing). It adds to the fullness of life, and helps make you who you are.

The spiritual body

This body is about connection. When we work with it, we open ourselves up to a deeper connection with our true Self – that's the self at our core: that steadiness and peace that exists within us, always.

The cosmic body

Most of us experience the cosmic body at some point without even realizing it. It's the level at which we go *beyond* the self and feel our connection with everything. Maybe you've felt it: sitting in nature and sensing the world spinning beneath you, knowing that you're a part of something bigger; feeling love (or you know, just a normal level of warmth and kindness) for a stranger on a train, for no reason; looking up at the stars and appreciating how small you are – in a liberating, wonderful way.

The nirvanic body

This body is where we experience ultimate freedom. A true sense of liberation – nothing in the world can keep us down, or hold us back from being who we are. When you work regularly and closely with this body you can feel free in any moment, no matter what's going on around you. That feeling of freedom will come and go, but it's *always* possible.

Trauma doesn't exist in a vacuum – it affects all seven of our bodies. And because each body plays a part in how we feel, move, breathe, act, and live, inner healing cannot take place if only *one* body is healed. We have to work with all seven, and allow new connections to form between them.

You get the point: We're going to work with these bodies one by one, going deeper into the self and healing each layer as we move through it.

And now... forget everything I've just told you (well, sort of).

You don't need to keep the seven bodies in your head. Trust that you're doing the work by reading the book. There's no need to get caught up in the bodies, or identify with them too closely, because this book will guide you through them effortlessly. Think of it as a concept that helps us approach inner healing in a purposeful way. The bodies, or layers of the self, don't need to become a concrete reality in your mind; we're simply using them as a framework to help us explore ourselves more fully.

What does inner healing look like?

When I talk about self-healing, I'm often asked what that actually looks like in real terms. And it's a really tough question to answer. I don't want to tell you exactly how you should feel, or what outcome you should aim for, because there's no 'should' about it. Different people feel different things, and need different things, and experience different changes and growth patterns as they delve deeper into their inner work.

I guess this is a bit of a disclaimer. But here are some general effects you can expect along the way. Read them with the awareness that your journey is unique to you. If you don't experience any of these things, or if you experience a whole host of completely different things, it doesn't mean you're doing it wrong (or that there's anything wrong with you).

You may find that you:

- Feel a new emotional stability and have greater control over your reactions and responses to the things that trigger you (or those triggers will seem to disappear completely).
- Experience a deep sense of self-acceptance.
- Feel peaceful. Inner peace isn't easy to come by. It really does take work – but you'll do that work as you read this book. You'll get there.
- Gain a new ability to look back on hurtful situations without feeling the pain all over again. Every single time.
- Overcome negative behavior patterns that developed following traumatic experiences or events.

Trauma doesn't exist in a vacuum – it affects all seven of our bodies. And because each body plays a part in how we feel, move, breathe, act, and live, inner healing cannot take place if only *one* body is healed. We have to work with all seven.

- Let go of your 'limiting beliefs' – the unconscious beliefs you hold about yourself and the world that limit the way you live your life – and create a new set of beliefs that make you feel empowered, positive, and full of hope.
- Face your inner child, and heal wounds that you sustained years ago.
- Break the cycle of generational trauma – so the things that have hurt you won't hurt future generations of your family or community.
- Feel free.

How to use this book

You'll need a notebook and a pen or pencil, and a desire for growth and change. I've designed this book to be used in two ways:

1. First, work through it step by step, from the beginning to the end. Because each chapter builds on the previous one, and each exercise builds on the last, it's a journey in itself. When you reach the end of this process you'll have taken huge steps toward healing yourself. But everyone's journey is different, and there'll always be loops in the path and potholes in the road.

2. Second, when you've worked through the book once, go back and reread the chapters that you feel called to work on more. Use the practices that feel most helpful to you again and again. Redo them; rework them. Each time you use one of the practices, write it down in your notebook – so you can measure your progress over time and see how far you've come.

Keep this book on your desk, or by your bed, or in your bag. Return to it when you feel triggered or overwhelmed and need to be reminded of how to ground and steady yourself. And whenever you lose your way and can't see the path clearly ahead of you, come back. Read. Settle. Breathe.

There's no such thing as failure. No matter how many times we fall down, we can always get back up again.

Now, let's do it.

Each of the chapters that follow is centered on one of the seven bodies. In this way, the book builds gently and sequentially. You'll move deeper into your self, and explore subtle parts of your human experience.

Enjoy the journey – it might just change your life.

CHAPTER 2

Start with the body you know

The physical body holds our pain – but it can also be the key to releasing it.

We begin our journey through the seven bodies with the one we're most familiar with. Let's start with a question: What's your relationship with your physical body like?

I hope that there's some love, appreciation, and positivity there, but you wouldn't be alone if you *did* have some worries about your body. In fact, if you've been through any kind of traumatic experience in your life, it's probably settled into your physicality somewhere – stored away and remembered so that you can feel it when you walk, or run, or bend, or breathe, or lie still.

The hardest moments of my life were mapped in my body. And when I went through that breakup, the pain I felt wasn't only emotional. Walking down the street I'd see something that reminded me of my ex – a woman dressed in clothes similar to those she'd worn, or a couple arguing, which she'd have commented on, whispering conspiratorially in my ear – and my heart would pound. My chest would tighten and it'd become hard to breathe, and then I'd feel sick. My legs would suddenly get heavy, and I'd find it harder to walk; I'd seem to forget how to move my limbs in harmony with one another.

That physical intensity was always quickly joined by emotional distress, and I'd feel hopeless. How could I move on if there were reminders of her everywhere, and if my body wouldn't allow me to walk past those reminders without disintegrating into panic and despair?

If the traumatic event you experienced was largely physical, your body's reaction to triggers may be even more debilitating. When someone or something hurts us, the physical body holds on to that pain. We don't just let it go the moment the experience is over. We *can* let it go, later, but doing so takes awareness, willingness, and effort.

Work with the physical body to kick-start healing

A few years ago, I worked with a coaching client who wanted to establish more positive routines and habits in her life. Her main goals were to get fit and to get out more; she felt she'd become reclusive and had developed anxiety in relation to going out and socializing. She wanted to feel confident and happy, and enjoy spending time with other people.

We agreed to start by combining the two goals, and she signed up for a workout class that had a sociable vibe – the participants usually went for a drink together after each session, and also met up in the park at weekends for extra workouts. It seemed like a simple way to kill two birds with one stone, with the structure and support my client needed to feel comfortable about putting herself out there.

And yet, as the weeks went on, she found the sessions more and more difficult. It wasn't the workouts themselves she was struggling with – although she'd felt niggles in her lower back and hips that developed into ongoing pain. Instead, for two full days before each session, she'd agonize over the post-workout drinks.

She'd call me and say, 'I can't stop thinking about it. I can't go. I don't know what I'll say, or what I'll do with my hands. And what about the walk from the gym to the pub? Who will I walk with? What if no one joins me and I'm walking alone, behind everyone else, like an idiot?'

'Why would that happen?' I'd ask.

'Why wouldn't it? I feel like this isn't the right plan. It's not working. I'm not feeling more confident.'

I'd reassure her that it was early days, but inside I was concerned; at that stage of a coaching program it was unusual for a client not to feel the force of possibility and hope, at least a little bit. I'd thought that the workout sessions would give her a soft landing: a low-pressure way to start putting herself out there. But it was so much harder for her than I'd expected, which led me to wonder if she'd given me the full story.

So, for the second time, I asked her: 'When do you think you started to struggle with social situations?'

The phone line went silent for a while. Then, ignoring my question, she said, 'What if they don't really want me to come to the pub and they're just letting me tag along because it would be rude not to? But actually... they hate me?'

'Whoa! Let's rewind a little,' I said. 'Why would a group of relative strangers hate you? That's a very strong emotion. I'd bet that they're mildly curious about who you are and interested in having a chat and finding out a bit more. It's a low-key social gathering with a group of people who go to a workout class together – social politics are at a minimum there.'

When someone or something hurts us, the physical body holds on to that pain. We don't just let it go the moment the experience is over. We *can* let it go, later, but doing so takes awareness, willingness, and effort.

'I've always been hated.'

There. That was it. She'd said out loud the thing she'd been most ashamed of for years; the thing that she'd been carrying with her, secretly, hoping no one else would notice. I knew this was a pivotal moment in her journey and that I had to proceed carefully; if I said the wrong word, she could interpret that as *me* reinforcing this belief she had about being hated. And then there'd be no way I could help her – she'd walk away.

'OK,' I said, 'I respect that belief. I understand that it came from somewhere. And for us to move past this moment and find a way to get your confidence up, we need to talk about where it might have come from. Because – and I say this with kindness, I promise – it's very unlikely that it's true. You haven't always been hated. You're certainly not hated right now; I don't hate you.'

'Thanks...' she hesitated, and then went on: 'I used to have a really great group of friends. We met at school when we were teenagers and we stayed friends into our twenties. One of them... Well, I fell in love with one of them, and I thought he fell in love with me. And we got married when we were 25. We got together when we were barely 17 and we were together for 10 years, and the whole time I thought we were happy.'

She paused, and I said nothing; this was a time to practice listening, not a time to push.

'Then I came home one day and one of our friends was there. There were eight of us in this group, and she and I were as close as the rest – or I thought we were. I didn't get it to start with. She was in my living room in her underwear, holding the TV remote control in one hand and a drink in the other. I thought... well, I don't know what I thought. Then my husband walked out of the bedroom and he was... in his underwear too... and that was it. I knew.'

'He was cheating on you with your friend,' I said.

'Yeah. But this is the thing – the whole group knew about it. And they'd been doing it for years, since we were 18. They'd always been doing it, our whole relationship, our whole marriage, and I was the only one of the eight of us who didn't know. They'd all been in on it. So they hated me – that's all it could have been, for them to all... trick me.'

I heard her voice crack, so I told her to take some time to rest and relax. We'd meet and make a new plan the following day.

And I understood it – her struggle with being in a group of people, and her fear of being the one who was left out and judged and secretly shunned. It wasn't a fear of new people, or a fear of people at all – it was a fear that she wasn't good enough to be an equal part of something. She'd been pushed to the edges of something she thought was safe and loving, and she'd been *more* than betrayed. She'd been made to feel worthless.

She wasn't unusual in internalizing that – it'd be hard for anyone not to. It's hard not to internalize pain and blame when your partner cheats on you, but when a group of friends are in on it, and lying to you... How can you convince yourself that they were *all* doing something bad and not just behaving in the way that you *deserve*?

When my client and I met the next day, we decided to start small. 'For now, let's forget about going for the post-class drink,' I said, 'and focus on the class itself.'

So she did. She went to the class twice a week, and for a couple of months she didn't even entertain the idea of joining the group at the pub afterward. She just did the practical, physical thing, and then said her goodbyes and left. And the result of doing that surprised us both – the pain in her back and hips completely disappeared.

'It wasn't actual pain from the exercise,' she said, 'it was the fear of going out after the class. When I stopped feeling that, I stopped feeling pain.'

That was a huge moment in her personal healing journey. Not everything was solved right away, of course, but she experienced the physical power of her emotions and anxiety in a tangible way. And for me, it was an equally huge moment in my coaching work *and* in my own inner healing process. I'd read books and heard lectures about the way we store trauma in our bodies, but it hadn't been shown to me in such an unmistakably clear way before.

Not only was my client carrying that pain in a particular area of her body, but beginning to work *with* her body, *just* her body, started to release the emotional pain as well as the physical. Within weeks of attending those sessions and no longer feeling the physical pain, she started thinking again about going to the pub with the workout group – and found that she wasn't afraid. She'd worked on the physical first, and the emotional healing followed.

Of course, it took much more time to go deeper and get to a place where she genuinely felt strong, and confident, and worthy of love and respect. But the physical work kick-started the process, and acted as a key to unlock the door that led to her unique inner healing path.

What's your relationship with your physical body like?

Let's return to this question...

Don't get me wrong: I know this isn't an easy one to answer. While some of us do have an existing understanding of how we feel about our body, others have lived life up to this point absolutely determined not to accept that this relationship is complicated. I don't know about you, but I've never met anyone – either in my professional life or my personal life – who didn't have some kind of physical hang-up, *or* who felt completely comfortable with everything about the way their body looked, felt, and worked.

Because almost every experience we've ever had is recorded in our bodies. Some are present in obvious ways – like an injury or a scar sustained in a traumatic incident, or a way of moving that developed because of criticism or pressure to conform to a norm.

For example, I've a friend who walks with his feet turned outward in a way that looks pretty uncomfortable, and when I asked him about it once, he said that as a child, his grandparents had told him he was 'pigeon-toed' and made him correct it. Although his knee and hip joints have suffered ever since, he's never been able to let go of the deep-seated belief that if he walks with his feet turned inward, he's somehow not good enough.

Yet other experiences are present in much more subtle ways. A twinge of pain when we sit in a certain position; a rigid belief that our bodies are incapable of doing something; a digestive issue connected to stress; a fear of our bodies looking a particular way to other people, or a fear of our bodies being seen at all.

So, because I know it's not an easy question, I don't expect you to come up with the answer just by thinking about it. Instead, I'd like you to settle into the first practical exercise in this book – a practice that will begin to prepare you for everything that comes later. It's a way to ask your *whole* body, instead of your brain alone, how it's doing, and to acknowledge discomfort where discomfort exists.

Practice #1: The personal history body scan

Body scan exercises are used in all kinds of bodywork methodologies (including yoga and different schools of meditation), and with good reason. The science behind such methods has been explored in more depth over the last decade or so, and it's become blindingly clear that the benefits of body scan-based practices aren't just spiritual pseudoscience.

Experts from different fields, including psychology and neuroscience, have found that exercises similar to the one I share later can have powerful outcomes: from treating insomnia[6] to easing the effects of stress, depression, anxiety disorders, and even post-traumatic stress disorder.[7]

This particular body scan technique will do the following:

- Create an overall experience of deep relaxation – and from there, you can feel the edges of your body and notice discomfort without being afraid of it.
- Help you learn to tell the difference between physical discomfort that's *only* physical (which I believe is very rare) and physical discomfort that's connected to emotional discomfort or trauma.
- Hone your ability to recognize patterns in the way you feel, so that over time, it gets easier to pin down exactly where in your body you're holding past experiences. In turn, this means you'll know which areas of the body to work with in order to release those experiences and progress along your inner healing path.

6 Datta, K. et al. (2017), '*Yoga Nidra*: An innovative approach for management of chronic insomnia – A case report': https://sleep.biomedcentral.com/articles/10.1186/s41606-017-0009-4 [Accessed January 2, 2021]

7 Dhamodhini, K. and Sendhilkumar, M. (2018), 'Outcome of yoga nidra practice on various mental health problems and general wellbeing: a review study': www.ijcmph.com/index.php/ijcmph/article/view/3979 [Accessed January 2, 2021]

When it comes to healing, awareness is key. You've got to be willing to *notice* what's going on with you, and it's crucial to develop tools that allow you to focus, become present, and acknowledge how you're doing in this moment.

- Feel close to your body and experience warmth and love toward it, instead of feeling detached from or distrustful of it.
- Act as a healing practice in itself. The experience of settling into your body and being present with it, and feeling the roots of your vibration and noticing where positive energy flows freely and where it doesn't, will help you to become more attuned with your body, and inner harmony will begin to unfold.

When it comes to healing, awareness is key. You've got to be willing to *notice* what's going on with you, and it's crucial to develop tools – like this one – that allow you to focus, become present, and acknowledge how you're doing in this moment.

Most body scan practices are done with the eyes closed – this is because closing the eyes helps to take attention away from our external senses and focuses the mind inward, on the internal experience. But this one can be done with the eyes closed or open – it's your choice.

I've designed the practice to work in this way because I understand that if you're dealing with certain forms or manifestations of trauma, closing the eyes can make you feel incredibly vulnerable (not in a good way) or trigger panic or emotional distress. And that'd be much more distracting than simply having your eyes open.

On top of that, an eyes-open practice means you can dip into these instructions as you go along, if you need to; then maybe, when you've got the hang of it, you can try this exercise with your eyes closed, if you feel comfortable doing so.

Map your history, physically

Find a quiet room where you won't be disturbed by anyone for a while. Make any adjustments you need to feel comfortable, secure, and calm in this room; perhaps by closing the door, opening a window to allow in fresh air if it's warm, or using a heater or blankets if it's cold.

And then you're ready to begin. Read the following instructions in full before you start the practice, but feel free to refer back to them during it if you need to.

1. Lie flat on your back with the legs wide apart and the feet dropping outward. Take your arms out to the side, with the palms facing toward the ceiling. If you feel pain or discomfort in the lower back when you lie like this, you can place a couple of cushions underneath your knees; alternatively, you can bend your knees and bring your

feet flat to the floor, close to your hips. Elevating the knees will release the lower back toward the floor.

2. If you wish to close your eyes for this practice, now is the time to do so. If you're keeping your eyes open, let your gaze soften so it becomes a little blurry, almost unfocused.

3. Make any final movements you need to make in order to feel completely comfortable here. If there's an itch, scratch it; if there's a niggle, stretch it out; if there's hair or clothing in your face or bothering you somewhere else, move it. And then, when you're ready, settle into stillness.

4. Starting at the feet, notice every part of the body in turn. You don't have to do anything at all. You don't need to move or change that part of the body as you notice it; just *notice* it. This is the practice of scanning the body. Work all the way through the body, in the following order:

   Notice the...

   ~ toes of the right foot

   ~ sole of the right foot

   ~ heel of the right foot

   ~ top of the right foot

~ whole of the right foot

~ right ankle

~ right shin, then the calf

~ right knee – front, then back

~ right thigh – front, then back

~ right buttock

~ right hip

Become aware of the whole of the right leg and foot.

Then notice the...

~ toes of the left foot

~ sole of the left foot

~ heel of the left foot

~ top of the left foot

~ whole of the left foot

~ left ankle

~ left shin, then the calf

~ left knee – front, then back

~ left thigh – front, then back

~ left buttock

~ left hip

Become aware of the whole of the left leg and foot.

Now, notice the...

~ lower abdomen

~ belly button

~ lower ribs

~ upper ribs

~ right side of the chest

~ left side of the chest

~ fronts of the shoulders

~ tops of the shoulders

~ backs of the shoulders

~ right fingers

~ right palm

~ right wrist and forearm

~ right upper arm

~ left fingers

~ left palm

~ left wrist and forearm

~ left upper arm

~ upper back

~ mid back

~ lower back

Wrap the awareness around the sides of the body – both sides of the waist. And then become aware of the whole torso. You're completely aware of the whole torso.

Now, notice the...

~ throat

~ chin, and jaw

~ mouth

~ right cheek

~ right ear

~ left cheek

~ left ear

- nose
- bridge of the nose
- right eye, and eyebrow
- left eye, and eyebrow
- forehead

Allow the awareness to travel upward still. Notice the top of the head. The back of the head. And then the back of the neck. You're aware of the whole of the head and the neck.

And then notice the whole body. From the tips of the toes to the top of the head, you're completely aware of the whole body. Relaxed, calm, and still. You're completely at ease.

5. Lying here with this focused, alert (and maybe even a bit blissful?!) awareness of the whole body, you're beginning to feel into your physical experience. You're connecting with your body. You're acknowledging the symbiotic relationship between every part of you and every other part of you.

   So now, become aware of your vibration – of the sensation of energy that's coming from your body. Notice that overall vibe; it might feel like a kind of heat, or a visceral pulsing energy, or it might feel more subtle – something you sense without any noticeable physical sensation. This relaxed, aware state is ideal for noticing where you're at, and whether your vibration is low, heavy, or slow, or high, vibrant, and flowing freely.

6. Then allow the awareness to travel to any areas in the body that don't feel quite 'right.' This will feel different for everyone. You might notice areas that feel tense, or uncomfortable. Or, as you move the awareness through the body in any direction that you feel called to move it, you might notice that you automatically avoid certain areas, or rush past them – because they trigger an uncomfortable emotion or memory.

   Focus on those areas. Again, there's nothing to *do* – just notice them. Allow the awareness to rest in those places. Acknowledge the feelings that exist there. Accept that there's something there that may need to be healed.

7. Finally, lay your hands on your chest with the palms facing downward. Thank yourself for working through this practice. And make a promise to your body by voicing the following phrase, aloud or internally in your mind: *I will give my attention to the areas that have asked for my attention. I will heal what needs to be healed.*

8. **Take a deep breath, and then when you feel ready, gently sit up. Take your time to transition out of this practice and into the rest of your day. There's no rush.**

Resistance is a clue

Any thought, emotion, sensation, or experience that you try to resist or avoid exposes a space inside of you that's calling out to be healed (within reason, of course – it's normal and healthy to want to avoid objectively awful experiences). The exercise you've just worked through is a simple way to begin noticing that resistance, so that you can build a more solid understanding of what you can focus your inner healing energy on at any given moment in time.

In other words, you don't need to be scared of the things you feel a strong aversion to. Instead, you can welcome those things as clues, and aim to approach them with curiosity rather than fear. You'll probably find that shifting your approach in this way takes away their power surprisingly quickly.

The client I wrote about earlier in this chapter discovered that her physical pain held important clues that could help heal her emotional pain. And she's definitely not alone. In his eye-opening book *The Body Keeps the Score*, Dutch psychiatrist Bessel van der Kolk explores this subject in great detail. He says that after going through a traumatic experience, as much as we try to pretend that nothing's happened and get on with our lives as normal, 'the part of our brain that is devoted to ensuring our survival (deep below our rational brain) is not very good at denial.'

Long after a traumatic experience is over, it may be reactivated at the slightest hint of danger and mobilize disturbed brain circuits and secrete massive amounts of stress hormones. This precipitates unpleasant emotions, intense physical sensations, and impulsive and aggressive actions.'[8]

We do everything we can to *avoid* facing our trauma, but it's impossible to wipe it from our history. If we try to do that, or pretend to, it will always come back to bite us. Instead, we must *work* with it. Turn it over and look at it differently.

And gradually, over time, in a messy way that's by no means linear (there'll be good days and bad days – and there won't always be any obvious reason why we're suddenly stuck in the depths of a really,

---

8 Van der Kolk, B. (2015), *The Body Keeps the Score: Mind, Brain and Body in the Transformation of Trauma*. Penguin Books.

really bad day), we need to come to a kind of acceptance of that trauma as part of our past. *Then* we'll be healing.

In 2019, when my own healing journey was already well underway, and I'd firmly established my own practice of choosing curiosity over fear, I did something that wouldn't have been possible for me when I was younger. I remember the date because it felt huge: March 31 – Mother's Day in the UK.

I made an Instagram post sharing some of the struggles and trauma I went through with my family when I was a child. This trauma runs deeper than the breakup I told you about earlier. It'd shaped who I was (and still am), and it'd taken years and incredibly hard work for me to begin to accept that my childhood self – my inner child – deserved to speak out and be free.

In that post, I wrote about life after my father's death when I was very young. I wrote about my mother, the greatest strength in my life, and how she struggled to settle into a new country and a new language on her own with us kids. I wrote about the abusive in-law we lived with, who pushed his pain on us – sometimes violently. And I shared with the world how we'd feared for our lives, faced racist abuse, been homeless and lost, and gone hungry.

We do everything we can to *avoid* facing our trauma, but it's impossible to wipe it from our history. If we try to do that, or pretend to, it will always come back to bite us. Instead, we must *work* with it. Turn it over and look at it differently.

We were outsiders, and I carried sadness and fear with me for years as a result of everything we'd endured. The intensity of those emotions would come out whenever I felt as if I didn't fit in, or as though I was being rejected. I'd feel it in my gut, in my heart, in the stiffness that sank into my joints, and in my body's unwillingness to stand tall and broad and take the big, confident steps that I so wanted to take.

However, by the time I made that post, I'd also realized that I carry something else from that time. Something even more powerful: the strength, faith, and perseverance that my mother demonstrated to us every single day. And which even *I* demonstrated to myself, by simply surviving – because when I acknowledged what I'd been through and what I'd moved past, it was impossible not to acknowledge that I was also strong, and that I'd grown from something solid. Even though our lives were unstable, our hearts were not.

Trauma never gives you only one thing. If you look closely, there's always evidence of a truth beneath the lies that your pain wants you to believe. Because you've survived – you're a survivor.

You can use your body to start the process of accepting emotional pain that stems from the early years of your life. Your body is a tool that's with you all the time, if you just learn how to use it. Moving your body in certain ways can kick-start the process of inner healing – giving you an opportunity to go back to a time *before* you were hurt; and to feel into your physicality as if it were new, and as if the possibilities of your life were untainted, blank, and wide open. Which is a kind of truth in itself because the possibilities of your life *are* wide open.

John Stirk, a prominent UK yoga teacher, has for years dedicated himself to studying the way people move, and why. When I read his book *The Original Body*, I was inspired by the idea of moving our bodies as if we've never moved them before.[9] If you were completely new to the world, how would you experiment with this body you were born with? What would your muscles do? Where would your eyes glance?

The way we choose to move and the decisions we make about how to use our bodies – and how to change, or at least momentarily interrupt, movement patterns we've stuck to for years – has a powerful impact on the way we feel. Moving your body in a new way can allow your mind to move in a new way.

That's what I'd like you to try now.

9 Stirk, J. (2015), *The Original Body: Primal Movement for Yoga Teachers*. Handspring Publishing Ltd.

Practice #2: Move, shift your energy, and make space for your potential

For this exercise, you need to feel comfortable in your surroundings. You don't require much physical space, but you do need headspace. That means no interruptions. No worry in the back of your mind that someone might walk through the door any minute and ask what you're doing. Because you need to feel unselfconscious, and able to... well, be a bit weird, basically.

We're going to work with the body as if it were new. Later, we'll go deeper into connecting with what's known as the 'inner child' and 'reparenting,' to create new neurological pathways and release the unconscious limiting beliefs about yourself that are holding you back. This physical practice lays the groundwork for that – establishing a new perspective in the physical body.

And you know what? This might feel really strange. It might be uncomfortable for you, and you might feel strong resistance to it. All of that's OK. It *is* a bit strange. However, you don't have to believe in it right away for it to work. It's a practice. It uses the physical body. And even if you don't immediately experience any noticeable effects, it *is* working and you *are* doing it right.

The truth is, self-healing is chaotic. Sure, there'll be minutes, days, weeks, even months when you'll feel a kind of joyful harmony and your progress will be obvious. But for much of the time, healing feels icky. Sometimes it hurts. A lot. Because it has to. Be patient with your emotional wounds.

Expand and sense

When you've decided on your quiet, undisturbed place, and you know you have 10–15 minutes of peaceful alone time, you can get into this. Keeping your eyes closed until step 8 will improve the effectiveness of the exercise; however, if you feel uncomfortable with your eyes closed, then try softening your focus instead, perhaps by gazing at the floor or some other neutral point.

1. Sit with your back against a wall, your knees pulled into your chest and your feet flat to the floor. Cross your arms around your legs, and ball your hands into fists. Rest your head on, or near, your knees. If this feels uncomfortable or impossible, try placing a cushion on top of your knees and resting your head on that.

2. Close your eyes. Notice the breath. Don't try to change it or control it; just notice the breath. Each inhale and each exhale. Notice the length of the breath; the depth of the breath. Allow it to be as it is.

3. As you continue to rest here, notice these three points in the body: the forehead, the center of the chest, and the lower abdomen. Imagine that each of these three points is becoming softer, and warmer, and relaxed.

4. Take your time. And when you're ready, very, *very* slowly, begin to lift your head away from your knees. So *slowly*. As if you've never lifted your head before, and you're not sure how it works. You've never felt the muscles in your neck working, or experienced the sensation of air on the skin of your face. Keep the eyes closed. Keep lifting the head until it's balanced comfortably over the neck.

5. Next, and still with the eyes closed, begin to move the arms. Incredibly slowly. Again, it's as if you've never moved your arms before. They unfurl, uncross, and reach straight up over your head. And at some point, your hands relax and your fingers slowly stretch out straight, too. It's as if your arms are feeling their way out into the space around you for the very first time.

6. Now, gently tilt your head from side to side – still *very* slowly – first dropping the right ear toward the right shoulder, and then the left ear toward the left shoulder. You're experimenting with your body. Feeling what it feels like to move it. Exploring the air around you.

7. Just as slowly as you raised them, draw your arms back down. Cross them around your legs again.

The truth is, self-healing is chaotic. Sure, there'll be minutes, days, weeks, even months when you'll feel a kind of joyful harmony and your progress will be obvious. But for much of the time, healing feels icky. Sometimes it hurts. Because it has to. Be patient with your emotional wounds.

8. Then, with the same curiosity – wonder, even; as if you've never opened your eyes and sensed the world with vision before – open your eyes. See the space around you as if it were an alien landscape. New. And in its newness it's *amazing*. Every detail of it astounds you.

You can move through these steps just once, or repeat them 3–4 times to lengthen and deepen the internal effects.

I won't tell you what you should feel as you do this practice because everyone will feel something different. But regardless of whether the impact is obvious to you or not, the practice will almost immediately start to...

- Move and release energy. By moving as if for the very first time, you unstick and unblock the body. You move without the inhibitions you've picked up over your life so far, and instead explore and expand outward with pure sensing and pure curiosity.
- Release tension. You imagine that your body is new to the world. So there's no tension to hold, and signals travel from your brain to every cell of your being, inspiring total release and relaxation.

- Create physical space. You consider your body in a new way. For the duration of this practice, you wipe it clean – it becomes a blank slate. And that new physical space will continue to expand as you move through this book; ready to be filled with the new experiences and ideas that are to come.

Use this exercise regularly. Make it part of your daily or weekly routine, and each time you do it, allow yourself to do it with curiosity. There's always more to discover.

CHAPTER 3

What's your vibe?

Working with the etheric body will change your vibration and create love and trust.

Place a hand on your heart.

Take a deep breath.

How do you feel?

What do you need today?

Where's your head at?

And on a scale of *Ugh, I feel terrible and I want to hide away* to *I feel alive and excited about the potential of my future*, how is your *energy* flowing?

Your vibration, your vibe, is important. It's the energy that courses through you, and that you radiate out into the world; and by extension, it's the same energy that you welcome back. What you give more or less equates to what you receive, so getting familiar with your vibration is an important part of inner healing work.

If you're hurting, you're more likely to attract people who are hurting. If you don't believe in your own worth, others won't treat you as if you're worthy of genuine love and respect. If your vibe is low, heavy, and dark, it will be difficult to draw toward you people and experiences that are vibrating higher, lighter, and brighter.

In my first book, *Good Vibes, Good Life*, I wrote a *lot* about vibrations. At the center of it all is the idea that loving yourself is the key to vibrating on a higher level, and thus changing your life for the better. If you'd like to know more about manifesting that love for yourself and managing your vibration, I humbly recommend you explore that book. It's full of practices that cultivate self-love by caring for yourself: by meditating, eating well, drinking water, changing your body language, experiencing the present moment, and more.

Self-care practices are essential to healing, and I'll expand on developing a self-care routine later in the book. Nevertheless, it's important at this stage that you're engaged in things that you enjoy and that make you feel supported. Even if they're as simple as listening to music, going for walks in nature, speaking to a trusted friend, practicing yoga, or taking a bath.

In this chapter, however, I want to focus specifically on how your vibration affects your relationships, and how the vibe of the people you surround yourself with can impact on your capacity for healing.

Your vibration, your vibe, is important. It's the energy that courses through you, and that you radiate out into the world; and by extension, it's the same energy that you welcome back.

The physical techniques we worked through in the previous chapter have already created space and time for you to start noticing where your vibration is at – and it's relatively simple to figure out whether you're vibrating high, low, or somewhere in the middle. If your vibration is high and tuned in with the powerful positive energy that courses through the Universe, you just *feel* good. You feel confident. To others, it seems that you have a glow about you and that success and light come to you easily. You wake up in the morning and feel alive with the potential of the day ahead.

Creativity flows, good ideas strike without much trouble, and you manifest the things you want most in your life. Essentially, things go well. And when they don't, you feel the force of resilience and trust that everything's happening as it should and you'll soon be in a better, happier, stronger position.

However, vibrating on a high level is more difficult when you have lots of baggage to work through. This doesn't mean you can't do it, only that it will take more effort. That effort is absolutely worth it though because when you can raise your vibration during your inner healing work, it becomes much easier to accept trauma, move through pain, and confront challenges with a kind of steadiness – because you know that this will pass. You know, deep in the core of your being, that you're worthy of feeling better.

So, how do you know if your vibration needs to be raised? Start with how you feel when you wake up in the morning and go from there. If you're struggling to see the light at the end of the tunnel, and are feeling generally low and slow and tired, then your vibration is probably suffering. You're tapping into the heaviness and darkness out there – and by doing so, you're inviting more heaviness and darkness into your life.

Hold up! I promised I wouldn't ask you to suspend your disbelief while reading this book, and yet here I am talking about tapping into the energy of the Universe. I hear you. But whether you look at it from an esoteric perspective or you're more determinedly grounded in science, the Universe is made of energy. Quantum physics tells us this. We're made of energy. The Earth and the stars are made of it; and we're a part of it.

When we're born we're given this vessel, this body, with which we can use, shift, and express our energy. So, when it comes to getting to know your vibe and figuring out what your energy is up to, you don't have to become a super-spiritual green smoothie-guzzling type (although if you ask me, green smoothies are pretty good... give them a chance). Think of it, instead, as learning a new language – the language that will allow you to understand how you live in the world, and to change your energy so that your life can become happier and more fulfilling.

Taking charge of your inner healing is one of the greatest acts of self-love. By committing yourself to this process, you're already lifting your vibration and creating space to welcome more joyful experiences.

The importance of positive relationships

Let's get on to relationships, because they're an integral part of inner healing. If your relationships are positive and supportive, healing will happen faster and in a deeper, more sustainable way. However, if you're surrounded by people who bring you down, it will be much, much harder to lift yourself up.

In one way or another, almost all the trauma we carry with us is associated with a person or people. It's not that trauma is always something that's *done* to us or *caused* by other people – although it often is – but that those we spend time with during or after a traumatic experience have an immeasurable effect on how we manage our emotional pain. The relationships we have at any given time can do one of three things:

1. Inflict further damage, or create a hole of guilt, blame, and despair that convinces us we're going to be stuck forever.
2. Create a sense of emptiness, loneliness, or pointlessness; this is when a relationship doesn't do any harm, but it doesn't do any good either.

3. Lift us up and give us the confidence and motivation to confront our trauma and move through it with a sense that we're held and supported.

And this has as much to do with vibration as it does with explicit actions. If your vibe jars with the vibe of the people closest to you when you're going through something difficult, or when you're working hard to heal, you feel that vibrational conflict in everything you try to do.

What kind of people are you surrounded by right now? What kind of energy do they put out? Who have you tended to connect with over the years, and how have those connections affected you? And, importantly – who was close to you when you went through a significant traumatic event in your life?

I'm going to share the story of Malika (not her real name). She agreed to make her journey public in this book, but with the assurance that her identity would be protected; therefore, I've been cautious when describing the specific details of her experience.

Malika had a normal childhood and became a normal teenager with a normal family. They were supportive, she told me, but not particularly switched on when it came to trauma and recovery.

Like many families, they had a resistance to accepting that anything bad could happen to them, and preferred to sweep problems under the carpet, rather than look their deepest fears straight in the eye. But all that wasn't much of an issue in Malika's life. She didn't have anything huge that she needed help with... until she turned 15.

Not long after her 15th birthday, Malika was violently raped by a stranger. She'd been at a party and had gone home on her own; her parents and siblings were away for the weekend. Someone followed her there and then raped her. This violation would change Malika's perception of the world – and of other human beings – for the rest of her life.

After the rape, Malika didn't move for a day and a half. She lay on a rug on the ground floor of the house, with a blanket from the sofa pulled over her, and kept still. She said she might have drifted in and out of sleep during that time, but mostly she was acutely aware of being awake, and being in pain, and feeling utterly terrified.

She didn't do anything because she didn't know if there *was* anything she could do. She was in shock, and her thoughts had nothing to do with logic or regular awareness. 'I embodied fear,' she said. 'It was what I was. I was just fear.'

Taking charge of your inner healing is one of the greatest acts of self-love. By committing yourself to this process, you're already lifting your vibration and creating space to welcome more joyful experiences.

When Malika's parents arrived home, that's how they found her: on the floor, awake, and in pain. She doesn't remember much about the weeks that followed, but she knows that in the first instance, her parents took her to the bathroom, washed her, and asked her what had happened; after she told them, they tucked her into bed and left her alone.

'There was never any mention of going to the police,' she said. 'That wasn't something I would have thought of and... I don't know why my parents didn't. It just wasn't something that anyone considered. Maybe they feared being judged if the story had gotten around. Maybe they just didn't know how to cope with it.'

Then, as the initial shock began to subside and the physical injuries started to heal, Malika was able to begin the long and difficult process of healing emotionally from this highly traumatic event. She didn't tell anyone else about it, and nor did her parents. And they didn't talk about it together, either – at least not explicitly.

'In their attempt to be supportive, they'd ask how I was and say things like, "It's time you got out there. You need to learn that people aren't all bad. You need to get it into your head that the world isn't this dangerous place you think it is,"' Malika recalled.

'And I'd just... say nothing. I was deeply, deeply depressed and scared of everything. They were the only people I had for support, and I know they were trying, in their own way. But it wasn't the kind of support I needed. I didn't need to be told to get on with things, and I really didn't need them to pretend nothing had happened. Not that I knew what I *did* need. I just... I was hurting so much, and I was ashamed. Of course, my parents were deeply concerned that I was becoming distant from the world, and more withdrawn. They'd never been taught how to cope with such a devastating situation.'

Malika spent the next decade on an emotional rollercoaster. When she did eventually 'get back out there,' she did so with the wrong people. She used drugs, alcohol, and bad relationships to numb her pain, and all the while her family became increasingly frustrated by her failure to become the kind of daughter they'd assumed she'd be. At no point were her parents able to see that her behavior and her struggles were connected with the rape. They thought they'd given her everything she could possibly need in life, and that she was throwing it back in their faces.

Malika's parents inadvertently inflicted further damage on her. I'm not trying to lay blame, but this story is a powerful way to illustrate how damaging a lack of appropriate empathetic support can be. If the people supporting Malika had known how to help her look at her trauma head on, and accept the emotions she felt around it, and support her patiently, without pressure... Well, her journey to healing would have been very different. There's no doubt about it.

Luckily, she did find people who'd do that. When she was 26, she finally came to the conclusion – completely on her own – that she needed professional help. She started therapy. And then, when she felt strong enough, she embarked on a mind coaching process to build new, more positive habits into her life. And one of the important things that all this work enabled her to do was to surround herself with new people; to fill her life with those whose vibrations matched the person she wanted to be, the confidence she wanted to have, the freedom she wanted to feel, and the strength she already had inside of her. Her authentic self had become buried under the trauma she'd experienced, and was waiting to be reclaimed.

When something traumatic happens to you, or near you, there's no going back to the way things were before. You can't pretend that because of who you are, or the kind of childhood you had, or the kind of parents you have, or how much money you have, or whatever it is, that this kind of thing *doesn't* happen to people like you, and so it *can't* really have happened to you. This would just be the powerful force of denial.

That goes for all kinds of trauma – not only dramatic, terrifying incidents, but also more subtle ones. So often, I speak to people who say things like: 'I feel that my parents just preferred my brother to me. But that can't be true because that's not the kind of people they are – they wouldn't do that, so it must be my fault that I feel this way.' Or, 'I remember being really scared of my uncle, and I get this sinking, sick feeling in my stomach whenever I see his face, even as an adult. He used to hit me... But he's a kind person, so he must've had a good reason. Or maybe I just made it all up.'

The things that have happened to you, and hurt you, are *not* your fault. It's not your fault that you were born into the circumstances you were born into, or that someone chose to abuse their position in your life, or that you were in the wrong place at the wrong time.

The trauma isn't your fault. You may know this intellectually but still have a hard time accepting it in your gut. It's important to replace those negative beliefs with a positive affirmation, such as: 'I did the best I could and I'm safe now.' You can't change your past, but you can *choose* to make your future a lighter place. Here's the thing – *it's your responsibility to heal yourself.*

And one way you can do that right now is to start doing what Malika did, eventually – surround yourself with people who vibrate with the positive, beautiful power of universal energy. Give yourself permission to be lifted up, instead of believing that you deserve to be dragged down.

Practice #3: Instead of wondering what people think of you, consider what *you* think of *them*

It's time for this chapter's practical exercise. Unlike the others we've done so far, this is something to begin practicing now, on your own. But you'll then need to take it out into your life and practice it every time you have any kind of encounter with another person. I know that sounds like a *lot*. But actually, this exercise is small. It's a small shift in perspective which, when you do it regularly, will add up to a much bigger shift.

This exercise is rooted in a technique that's often used in psychotherapy and Neuro-Linguistic Programming (NLP) work, and it allows you to start experiencing life from *your own* viewpoint. When you do this often, you'll start to look at the world from the inside out, rather than constantly trying to see yourself from other people's point of view. Which, in turn, will increase your confidence and self-esteem.

You can't change your past, but you
can *choose* to make your future
a lighter place. Here's the thing –
it's your responsibility to heal yourself.

It will create a steadier foundation of selfhood and worthiness, and a willingness to trust your own feelings and wishes instead of first worrying about what other people think of you. This works on a vibrational level too, because instead of trying to fit yourself into other people's ideals, you'll begin to consider how another person's vibration affects your own (if at all).

When you meet someone new, or even when you spend time with someone you already know well, what's your focus? Do you find yourself wondering what they think of you? Worrying about how they're interpreting your words, your movements, and general being? Do you spend hours after meeting someone new agonizing over whether or not you made a good impression?

You're not the only one. We're social animals and we crave social connection. We desire the feeling of being liked and wanted. And on top of that, those of us whose thoughts about ourselves have been affected by some kind of trauma are even more likely to try to be liked, to fit in, and to shape ourselves into what we think other people want us to be.

This makes us feel safer because it takes the vulnerability out of our social encounters and relationships. However, it also keeps us low. It stops us from expressing our true Self and from feeling comfortable with who we are. And ultimately, it actually holds us back from having truly fulfilling, deep, supportive relationships – because we're always hiding parts of ourselves and trying to be someone we're not.

Some psychologists suggest that always thinking about what *other* people think of us is also a sign of unhealthy perfectionism.[10] It's not that it's bad to try to develop ourselves and become better people, but that trying to become better people only from *someone else's perspective* isn't good for our sense of self.

US author and shame expert Brené Brown writes that 'Healthy striving is self-focused: "How can I improve?" Perfectionism is other-focused: "What will they think?"'[11] In other words, striving to improve yourself in a way that's healthy and positive means striving to improve for *you*. If you're striving to improve in a way that *someone else* thinks you should improve – or not even that: in a way that you *think* someone else thinks you should improve – you're making yourself less important than them.

---

10 Reynolds, J.R. and Baird, C.L. (2010), 'Is There a Downside to Shooting for the Stars? Unrealized Educational Expectations and Symptoms of Depression': https://journals.sagepub.com/doi/abs/10.1177/0003122409357064 [Accessed April 4, 2020]

11 Brown, B. (2010), *The Gifts of Imperfection: Let Go of Who You Think You're Supposed to Be and Embrace Who You Are*. Hazelden Publishing. 'Guidepost #2', pp.55–62.

You're sending yourself the message that you're unworthy of feeling good just for yourself, and that as a human being, you're only valuable if that other person or those other people approve of you/what you're doing/the words you say/the way you look, etc. You're trying to be somebody else's perfect. And honestly... that's never going to happen. People hold different opinions and expectations and these are ever-changing.

Cultivating a strong sense of self and knowing your own worth are incredibly important for inner healing because you cannot stay on this path if you're doing it for someone else. Undoubtedly, others will benefit from your healing. It will make you stronger, more empathetic, and truer to yourself, and your powerful vibration will radiate out and enrich the lives of everyone around you. But that can't be the purpose of it.

You can't heal just for someone else or you'll lose your way, or give up, or take a turn that leads you somewhere you don't really want to go. You need to feel certain that you deserve to heal; that you're doing this for you. That every time you pick up this book and read a page, or step out of the front door with your chin up, or cry huge, infinite, gut-wrenching tears, the end goal is *you*. Connecting with you. Feeling good as yourself. Believing that you deserve the best life you can possibly live.

It's frustrating, sometimes, that a strong sense of self is so important for inner healing. I get it. Because trauma makes it really hard for us to have a strong sense of self – it turns 'self,' and even 'body,' into abstract concepts; we feel detached from who we are. Perhaps you tell yourself things like, *It doesn't matter how I feel inside, as long as it looks like I'm all good from the outside.* Maybe you don't really know what it'd feel like to feel good inside. Your pain has distorted your perception, making it difficult to imagine life through a more positive/healed lens.

But I'm here to tell you that you *are* capable of feeling good, and rediscovering a steady sense of who you really are. You're working on it. You're becoming your own healer. No, scratch that – you're *already* your own healer. Right now, you're just learning to use the tools that have been inside you all along.

From the inside out

Anyway, the practice... Read the following instructions a couple of times over first, and then let's do this.

1. **Close your eyes. Take a few deep breaths, filling your lungs with oxygen and then emptying them completely. Then allow your breath to return to its natural rhythm. Your body relaxes. You're here, in this moment.**

2. Imagine meeting a new person. Make them real – visualize every detail of them. What they look like. The clothes they're wearing. How they're standing or sitting. Imagine you can hear their voice as they say hello and start telling you about themselves.

3. Now imagine that as you listen to that person, you aren't thinking about what they think of you at all. You're not worrying about what your face is doing or how your hands are moving; you're not brushing your hair out of your eyes, or planning what you're going to say when they stop talking. You're just listening. Taking them in.

4. Then imagine telling the person something about yourself. Make it brief; maybe your name and one personal fact that you think defines you in some way. But imagine telling them this without any thoughts about how they'll respond to it, or what they'll think of you. Tell them something that *you* like about yourself – not something you think *they'll* like, based on what they've already told you about themselves.

5. The two of you say goodbye. You walk away.

6. Now imagine asking yourself, *Do I like that person?* Consider the question. Turn it over in your mind. The intention here isn't to be judgmental, but to be honest with yourself about what you think of that person. Did they give off a good vibe? Are they someone you'd

like to learn more about? Someone you'd like to be friends with? Did you feel any discomfort around them? Did you get a sense that they were trustworthy, or not?

7. Allow yourself to settle on a simple answer. *Yeah, I like them*, or *Nah, not really my kind of person*, or *Not sure – would be cool to get to know them better and see.*

8. And then notice your breath again. Still inhaling and exhaling in a natural, gentle rhythm. Bring your awareness fully to your breath, and then let go of all thoughts of your interaction with the person you met. It's happened, and it's over. There's nothing more to think about.

Open your eyes in your own time. Have a little stretch if you feel like it – reach your arms up overhead and lengthen your spine. Release the encounter. Let it go.

What just happened? In your imagination, you met someone. You spoke with them briefly. You considered whether or not you liked them. And then you went on with your day.

What didn't happen? You didn't wonder what that person thought of you. You didn't worry about whether they liked you or not. You didn't try to see yourself from their perspective. You just looked at *them* from *your* perspective. Took them in.

You experienced the encounter from within yourself – you didn't try to turn yourself into an out-of-body, all-seeing mind-reader, floating somewhere in the sky and looking down on yourself and assessing your performance. You were just you, meeting someone and thinking, *Yeah, I like them*, or *No, not really into them.*

Create authentic and vibrant connections

The next step is to do this in real life. When you're interacting with real people. This isn't about judging others, or becoming someone who speaks badly about people. Your impressions may well be positive, and either way, the intention here isn't to share your thoughts about this other person with anyone else. Instead, you're practicing using your intuition to feel out someone else's vibe, and to counter any tendency you may have to worry about what *they* think of *you* by focusing on your *own* experience of the interaction rather than theirs.

It won't be easy to do this straight away. You'll still worry about what other people think of you – probably a lot. Don't worry about that; definitely don't beat yourself up about it. This is a process, a healing journey. There's no quick fix, and it will all take time.

If you're striving to improve in a way that *someone else* thinks you should improve – or not even that: in a way that you *think* someone else thinks you should improve – you're making yourself less important than them.

But try it. Whenever you remember to, take a moment to pull that out-of-body assessor back down to Earth, get inside of your body and think about what you think of the other person, instead of what they think of you. It's a game-changer, I promise. And the more you do it, the easier and more natural it gets – until you start doing it without even trying to. It becomes normal to you to meet others as yourself, in your body, with the confidence to decide whether or not their energy resonates with yours.

As well as boosting your sense of self, this practice will open you up to more positive relationships. You'll become more focused on nurturing the relationships that *do* feel good to you – those with people who vibrate on a similar level to your own, or on a level that lifts you.

I'd like to make it clear that this *doesn't* mean rejecting people in your life who are struggling, or who depend on you or need your help. Sometimes our purpose is to offer our support and unconditional love to others, regardless of their current situation or vibration. But this *is* about allowing yourself to also give your energy to the people and relationships that give back to you just as much as you offer them.

It's also about *not* feeling pressure to build a relationship with anyone who seems to like you, *just because* they like you. This particularly applies to meeting new people – especially if you've ever put lots of energy into building a relationship simply because you crave someone's approval. When you begin to act on intuition, and realize that you don't need the validation of people who you don't naturally connect with, you'll begin to surround yourself with people you truly want to be around.

And that will open up far more opportunities for genuine love, and authentic connection, and unshakable trust. Which will help you every single day as you move along your path to inner healing. Because love and trust are non-negotiable. We need them. We cannot get better on our own, or by hiding away for the rest of our lives.

Yes, we need to do a lot of our healing work on our own; however, we also need to be able to talk freely, to cry in front of someone, to lay our broken heart bare and know that space will be held for us to put it back together again. None of us – not one single person – is born with the capacity to be alone and be healthy and happy.

Bad relationships may hurt us, but good ones? They make possibilities infinite. They're essential. And you *deserve* to have them.

CHAPTER 4

Go back in time

The astral body develops during childhood, but that doesn't mean it's set in stone. Now is the time to build a new relationship with your emotions.

What did you go through when you were a child?

What happened in your life that you were unable to understand – not because you weren't clever enough, or good enough, but because you were too young?

The experiences we have as children can literally change the structure of our brain. That can be a really good thing, with positive connections made all the time; but when we have a bad experience before our brain has developed sufficiently to understand and process it in a healthy way, structures and connections are built that affect us long into adulthood. As a result, the trauma you suffered during your childhood could be governing the way you handle experiences and your emotions right now.

One interesting study, published in 2019 in the *Journal of Affective Disorders*, found that childhood trauma can even affect the way adults make moral decisions. In particular, the researchers found that being neglected as a child is most likely to impair an adult's moral decision-making process, and male study participants who'd experienced trauma in childhood were more likely than female participants to find it 'acceptable to cause harm' by personal force.[12] Of course, not all people who were neglected as children go on to be harmful to others in their adult life. But the likelihood increases.

Although your childhood self may have been intensely impacted by traumatic experiences, leading to cognitive distortions that have lasted into adulthood, you can be liberated through healing, and the practices featured in this book can be key to this process.

Think of it this way... A child – let's call him Brian – is grieving following the death of an important person in his life. Brian's father tells his son that if he cries he's weak; it's time for him to start acting like a man, he says, or no one will love and respect him. He then walks out of the room.

---

12 Larsen, E.M., et al. (2019), 'Effects of childhood trauma on adult moral decision-making: clinical correlates and insights from bipolar disorder': www.ncbi.nlm.nih.gov/pmc/articles/PMC6287939/ [Accessed March 15, 2020]

The trauma you suffered during
your childhood could be governing
the way you handle experiences
and your emotions right now.

Brian receives several different important messages from this exchange. He learns that he's weak if he cries, that he can't be a 'man' if he cries, and that he isn't worthy of love or respect if he shows 'weakness' and doesn't fulfill his father's idea of what a man should be.

Brian grows up, and he starts to create a life for himself. The messages he got from his father settle into his subconscious mind as firm beliefs and he tries to live by them. He meets a woman, falls in love, and builds a committed relationship with her. And then, unexpectedly, Brian's father dies.

Brian can't help himself. He cries – in front of his partner, who holds him while he weeps huge heartrending tears. When he calms down a little he pulls back and looks at her. His deep-seated childhood beliefs that he's weak, unworthy, and 'not a man' if he cries scream through his mind, and in her eyes he sees disdain, disgust, and rejection. He perceives that his partner no longer loves him because he's let the wall down and she can no longer view him as a real man.

And, beaten down further by this new grief for the very man who forged his limiting beliefs, Brian can't take it. He's no longer able to look his partner in the eye, and he feels he has no option but to distance himself from her by asking for a break a short time later.

But really? There was no disdain in her eyes, only love, concern, and empathy. But Brian couldn't understand what was really there in front of him because all he could see were the beliefs that were painfully etched in his mind. If he'd done the work to acknowledge and release those beliefs he would have been able to accept her support and move through his grief with a caring partner by his side. But he'd never done that work – he'd never known how to, or even known that he needed to. He'd believed without question the lies that his childhood trauma had told him, and so he felt and acted on those lies, even as an adult.

Who's talking – intuition or trauma?

To understand why Brian, or anyone else, might feel emotion, or take action, based on limiting beliefs from childhood, let's discuss something I often work on with clients. I've talked about this on social media a number of times, so if you've been with me for a while this idea may already be familiar to you. We can begin with a question: Is your intuition or your trauma taking the lead?

Trauma tells us to avoid being hurt again, at all costs. And when trauma takes the lead in our emotional state and decision-making processes, it blocks our natural intuition. Trauma feeds the fearful, wounded aspect of the ego and drives us to make decisions based on that pain. In contrast, when intuition guides our decisions and communication, we act from a place of love and steadiness.

Everyone has intuition. Yes – including you. From a psychological perspective, intuition is an innate ability to piece together snippets of information and emotional impressions to form a 'gut feeling' about something or someone. Famously, the great physicist Albert Einstein said, 'I believe in intuitions and inspirations... I sometimes feel that I am right. I do not know that I am.'

Psychologists recognize intuition as a non-analytical thought process[13] that happens mostly without our awareness, and it forms part of the overall process of making a judgment. If you've ever had a 'hunch,' or felt certain of something without really being able to explain why, that's your intuition.

Other perspectives on intuition draw on ideas about the Higher Self, or the true Self (we'll talk more about this later). There's a sense of knowing that comes from beyond the thinking mind; it has more depth to it. Some people feel that their intuition is rooted in

---

13 Zander, T., et al. (2016), 'Intuition and Insight: Two Processes That Build on Each Other or Fundamentally Differ?': www.frontiersin.org/articles/10.3389/fpsyg.2016.01395/full [Accessed January 10, 2020]

past-life experiences, while others tap into a knowledge that can't be measured by science. An inner confidence that something quite profound within them simply knows what it needs, wants, or is.

But although we don't notice when our intuition is putting things together and coming up with an intuitive answer to a problem or a choice, intuition *can* be clouded. Because when we're caught in a state of fear or trauma, we sometimes mistake the messages that trauma is sending us for something wiser. We think the fear-based messages are our intuition, when in fact they're created by unhealthy conditioning and are quietly disguising themselves as our deeper truth.

So, a useful way to start becoming more aware of childhood trauma, and the limiting beliefs that were created for you and still affect how you live and feel today, is to learn how to tell the difference between intuition-based and trauma-based emotions, decisions, and beliefs.

Great, but how exactly do you do that? When you're faced with a decision, a relationship, an emotional state, or anything else that triggers a strong reaction, take the time to sit back and work out whether your response to it is being led by intuition or trauma.

Intuition-based responses

A choice, feeling, or response guided by intuition usually comes with these qualities:

- A calm sense of knowing.
- A feeling of freedom, or being liberated.
- An undramatic and straightforward voice.
- No intense need to justify yourself with logic.
- A lighter heart, and a sense that your mind has lit up.
- Awareness and steadiness. You feel that you're here, in the present moment.
- A protective, guiding, and supportive tone.
- A clearer vision of the outcome or the future.
- The willingness to surrender to the unknown.

Trauma-based responses

In contrast, a choice, feeling, or response guided by trauma and fear will be more like this:

- An anxious and fearful assumption or judgment.
- A feeling of being limited or trapped.
- A dramatic, even frantic, voice.
- An intense need to prove the logic and rationality behind your response.
- A feeling that your heart is sunken, and your mind is dark or gloomy.
- Focused on the past – and perhaps using the past to justify your response.
- A restrictive and demanding tone.
- Feelings of being lost and confused.
- Resistance to the unknown; the sense that you must stay in control.

When you begin to acknowledge those moments in which you're being guided by trauma and fear, you're a big step (or a few big steps) closer to letting go of your limiting beliefs. You start to accept that what your childhood self thought about the world wasn't necessarily based on truth. And *that* is truly liberating.

If Brian had done this work, he might have been able to notice his trauma talking when he felt ashamed and unworthy because he'd cried in front of his partner. And that simple act of noticing could have changed his entire future.

What could change about *your* future if you were consistently led by calm, present moment intuition rather than guided by trauma and fear?

Any kind of trauma may have an impact on us, but early childhood trauma is arguably the deepest and most difficult to release.[14] After my first book was published, I spoke to countless readers about how difficult it was for them to start loving themselves. I found that for the majority of people, the hardest thing was letting go of the past.

Early life trauma created emotional instability in you at a time when you were still becoming you; you were developing, growing, and your development absorbed pain and fear and wrapped up that trauma tight. It might have created a void that you're constantly trying to fill, or fabricated an intangible monster that you're always trying to run from.

---

14 Heim, C. and Binder, E. (2012), 'Current research trends in early life stress and depression: review of human studies on sensitive periods, gene-environment interactions, and epigenetics': https://pubmed.ncbi.nlm.nih.gov/22101006 [Accessed February 26, 2020]

Trauma feeds the fearful, wounded aspect of the ego and drives us to make decisions based on that pain. In contrast, when intuition guides our decisions and communication, we act from a place of love and steadiness.

That's why, as difficult as it might be (and I promise, I'm right with you; this has been incredibly challenging for me, too), we can't ignore childhood trauma when we're working on our inner healing. If we did, we'd never really get there. We might patch up the emotional wounds we sustained more recently and feel, at least for a little while, that everything's under control and we're stronger and calmer. However, the childhood stuff *always* comes back – even if it was subtle, and even if we don't really identify with the term 'childhood trauma.' Because no matter who you are and where you've been, you *do* have limiting beliefs that you developed when you were very young.

Negative childhood experiences exist on a spectrum that ranges from mild forms of mistreatment to chronic and severe abuse. However, the main point is that healing is possible and one's outlook on life can radically change for the better. No one's life has been perfect. And that's OK. It's just a kind of acceptance that everyone is human; that no one gets through their early years completely untouched by the pain, insecurity, or fear of the adults around them.

But the good news is that it's possible to release those old beliefs and make way for new ones. It takes work, and it won't be easy – but you know that by now. And most importantly, you know that it will be worth the effort.

Practice #4: The personal history list

This is probably the hardest exercise I'll ask you to do. But you're ready for it – because by working through the previous chapters, you've already begun to recognize how and where you hold profound pain.

You've already created movement in your memories, in your history, and in the patterns you store in your body; so you've started to open up space that can soon be filled with more positive experiences and beliefs, and this exercise will increase that space infinitely. And you've learnt to look from the inside out and pay attention to what *you* think and feel, instead of trying to guess what *others* think and feel about you. Which means you've laid the groundwork to do this gently, and with love for yourself, and with a new awareness that the way you interpreted experiences and situations in the past may not have been true.

You're ready to confront your memories – the simple ones and the most challenging ones – and look at them from a new viewpoint. So it's time to write your list. This is a list of past memories, starting early in childhood, that have stayed with you and carry some strong emotional connection. Don't worry, you don't have to list them in chronological order – not many people's memories work like that – just write them down as they come to you.

The memories you're searching your mind for in this exercise are the ones that have really stuck... A comment from one of your parents that made you feel ashamed; a time you got something wrong and beat yourself up about it; the way a teacher treated you that somehow formed your ideas about how intelligent or valuable you are; the things you did with a teenage boyfriend or girlfriend; the way *you* treated someone else, which you've never quite forgiven yourself for; rejections; lies that you told, or believed; embarrassments; things you'd rather no one knows about you.

Search for trauma that you can easily identify as trauma, as well as those experiences that felt traumatic in some way, even if you can't easily identify them as such. Write down anything and everything that comes up – all of it.

You don't have to complete this exercise in one sitting. It might take time, so *give* it time. You can come back to it over the course of a few days or a week. Try not to leave more than a 20-hour gap between each time you sit down to work on it, though, because it's important to keep it moving; make sure the gaps are small enough that your brain keeps working on it. And when you feel like you've got to the end of your list, draw a line beneath it. Don't keep adding more and more memories once you've drawn that line. Just let it be.

Be aware that this exercise might hurt. That's completely normal. There's nothing wrong with you – no matter what you write on your list. It's also normal to feel shame, fear, and embarrassment as you work through this exercise. As I said, take your time, and have a break when you need to.

If you're currently working with a therapist and feel particularly intense emotions in response to this exercise, use your therapist. Talk it through. Ask for their support. Or reach out to a trusted friend instead. You don't have to share specifics; sometimes it's enough to say, 'I'm working on this really intense healing practice and it's shaken me up, could we go for a walk?' and ground yourself in the present moment again.

Make your list

Try to remember as you work through this exercise that there's a real purpose to it. It's leading to something beautifully positive – the opportunity, in the pages that follow, to shed the pain you feel and rewrite your beliefs in the way *you* want them to be.

1. Title your list. This makes it real and, somehow, makes it more likely that you'll see it through. The title is your call, and it doesn't have to be complicated. A simple 'memories list' would do the job.

2. Write your list. Start in early childhood, but remember you don't need to worry about putting everything in chronological order. Just write the memories as they come. You don't need to write loads of detail about each one; just enough so you know what the memory is. And make sure you number the list, so you can jot down the numbers of the most significant memories later on, if you need to.

3. Rate those memories on a scale from 1 to 10, with 1 being neutral and 10 indicating the most intense emotions. If you rate any of your memories above a 6 or a 7, I would strongly advise that you find and work with a mental health professional with specialized training and experience in trauma therapy.

4. Take breaks when you need to. Come back to it. See it through.

5. When your list is done, draw a line beneath it. Take in three deep, slow breaths through your nose and slowly let them out through your mouth. Letting go. Feel your feet firmly planted on the floor and imagine that outside yourself there is a safe, strong container that only you can open or close. Now, imagine opening the lid of that container and placing each memory that you've worked on today into the container and closing it so that the memory can be healed.

You've done the hardest part. If you'd like to learn more skills for managing painful emotions, I suggest finding a therapist trained in teaching a treatment called Dialectical Behavior Therapy (DBT).[15]

A few words about boundaries

Many of the people who haven't come to terms with their early life trauma have something in common: trouble setting healthy personal boundaries. (A boundary is a limit that helps the people around you understand how you want to be treated, and what is, and isn't, acceptable to you.)

This issue can manifest in lots of different ways, but particularly in how we manage our relationships. In all honesty, boundaries are hard for most of us. No one likes to disappoint other people; and someone who's really good at setting boundaries at work might not be so good at setting and maintaining them in their personal life.

It's important to understand that setting boundaries isn't a way to get rid of people, but a way to keep them in your life without destroying your inner peace. Healing doesn't mean rejecting the people in your life; but it does involve developing healthier, more

15 'Dialectical Behavioral Therapy', *Psychology Today*: www.psychologytoday.com/us/therapy-types/dialectical-behavior-therapy [Accessed January 8, 2021]

functional, and less triggering relationships with some of those people. Unfortunately, carrying limiting beliefs about who we are and what we deserve makes it even harder to be clear about what is – and isn't – acceptable for us.

My friend Sheena works in relationship mediation, and she once had a client who was struggling with one of those classic 'difficult relationships': the mother-in-law. The client – let's call her Paige – wanted her mother-in-law to feel welcome in her home, and the two of them got on pretty well. Everything was fine until Paige and her husband had a baby. Suddenly, Paige felt under a huge amount of pressure to let her mother-in-law see the baby whenever she wanted.

In the early days when Paige was recovering from giving birth and trying to get the hang of being a new parent, her mother-in-law would show up at the house without calling first, take the baby, and sit holding her for hours. Paige felt angry; she wanted time to adjust, to be with her new child, but her mother-in-law felt entitled to that time. Paige said nothing. She made the coffee, fed the baby when the baby needed feeding, and then allowed the baby to be taken from her arms again.

Fast-forward to a few years later and Paige and her husband decided to move to a new town. They'd both found work that suited

It's important to understand that setting boundaries isn't a way to get rid of people, but a way to keep them in your life without destroying your inner peace.

them there and were excited about the prospect of setting up a life that was truly their own. It wasn't too far from their families, but far enough that they'd have a bit more space. Paige figured that the unannounced visits from her mother-in-law would have to stop because she wouldn't want to drive 60 miles to find that no one was home. They weren't running away, but for Paige the distance was an extra benefit. She looked forward to enjoying her freedom.

And then her mother-in-law said, 'I'm going to move too. I've looked at a house for sale just down the road from you, and I've put in an offer. I'll be able to babysit all the time, and even pick up my granddaughter from school every day!'

Paige's heart sank. But she smiled and said nothing.

Paige was working with Sheena on a one-to-one basis because she knew she needed help with creating healthier boundaries in several different relationships. She relayed this new information to Sheena with an air of defeat. 'There's nothing I can do,' she said. 'I thought the distance would make life just that little bit easier, but she's just... she's going to move in next door. That's it.'

Sheena listened, and then asked Paige a seemingly simple question: 'During your life, have you ever had to make huge changes that felt completely out of your control? Has anything happened that you had no say in at all?'

Paige nodded without even a second's hesitation. 'Yeah, of course,' she said. 'When I was 10 my father moved in with this new girlfriend and I had to move in with them too. My mother couldn't cope with me anymore. I didn't want to, and I told my father that I wanted to live with just him, and not the girlfriend. He told me that if I didn't agree to live with his girlfriend then I'd have to be placed in foster care. If it was a choice between me or her, he'd choose her.'

Gradually, Sheena and Paige unraveled this even more. They talked about Paige's husband's role in the relationship between his wife and his mother; it turned out that the husband had barely been involved at all, and that his mother always went to Paige, not him, with her demands and wishes. Paige hadn't asked him for help in managing the situation. Why? Because deep down, she believed that if she asked him to choose between supporting her wishes and supporting his mother's wishes, he'd choose his mother. And Paige didn't want to go through that. She didn't want to push it, and risk being told that she was lower on his list of priorities.

So Sheena worked with Paige to build up her confidence around boundary setting. And just days later, Paige sat down with her mother-in-law and her husband, together, and gently explained that their new young family needed space to build their *own* life, and not be in the shadow of their parents all the time. Calmly and warmly, she reassured her mother-in-law that she was valued and loved but that they didn't need her to provide daily childcare; instead, they wanted her to enjoy special moments with her grandchild without being a daily fixture.

Paige's husband completely agreed with this; and although she was surprised and a little upset, her mother-in-law understood. A boundary was set – with love, kindness, and confidence.

Respecting your own boundaries

You, too, deserve to acknowledge your boundaries and communicate them clearly with the people around you:

- Are you a bit of an introvert who enjoys hanging out with people but needs private space to recharge at home? You deserve to tell your partner that inviting friends over three nights a week is too much for you, and have that need respected.
- Do you love going out and socializing but your partner prefers to stay in? You deserve to explain that you need a balance to be struck here, and that you want to go out and see friends on

your own when your partner doesn't want to come. Or, that you'd like your partner to come out sometimes, as this would be respectful of your needs and not only their own.

- Do you get stressed out when relatives rock up at your door unannounced? You deserve to explain that you're busy and need them to call ahead.
- Do you feel saddened that family members don't visit often enough, or call to see how you are? Maybe you need to let them know of this unmet need.
- Find it hard to say no to that friend who always asks for favors, or money, or emotional support, and never gives anything in return? You deserve to offer what you have to give on *your* terms, and step back when the friendship feels one-sided.
- Are you in a romantic relationship with someone who doesn't respect your need for honest communication? You deserve to ask for that, and be treated with understanding and kindness.

Whatever your needs are, you have to give yourself permission to explain them, ask for them to be respected, and expect that the people in your life will respect the boundaries that you set. If *you* respect your boundaries, others will too. And when you start to do that, you give yourself space to grow into your healing journey – because you're not constantly trying to deal with invasions of your personal space or emotional energy. You're protecting the space you need to heal and be well. You're also being clear about what you need more of from significant others, because this is setting a boundary around the absences or gaps that hurt you, and you're not willing to put up with this anymore.

A simple guide to setting boundaries

As I said, a boundary isn't a way of rejecting someone, or banishing them from your life – it's simply a limit that you set; and in turn, that limit sinks into your subconscious mind so you're better able to recognize and understand your own relationship needs. Boundaries protect our emotions, our personal space (literally and figuratively), and our vibration.

Boundaries also tell people with no uncertainty that you're no longer prepared to accept less – and that you won't put up with being neglected or forgotten. They're useful in all relationships, from professional to intimate, and are especially important with the people we love the most – because we're impacted more significantly by those we hold dear.

I'd like to make one thing clear: Boundaries aren't selfish and they're not cold. In fact, I'd suggest that they're the opposite – a firm but gentle, warm, and loving way to care for ourselves and others. Boundaries let us love ourselves more fully and offer ourselves respect. And of course, when we're comfortable with our own boundaries, we're also much better at noticing and respecting other people's boundaries.

When you establish healthy limits in your relationships, you give those relationships a space in which they can flourish and grow. You minimize the creeping discomfort and silent frustration that grows when a relationship demands too much from you or pushes forcefully into your personal space. Basically, boundaries make successful, loving, and healthy relationships possible.

Boundary setting in relationships

Here's a quick guide to setting boundaries in any relationship.

1. Take the time to notice which situations or interactions make you feel triggered. What does that person *do* that annoys you, upsets you, or makes you feel overwhelmed, unimportant, or overlooked? Also notice what you're feeling in your body when you're around the person who's difficult. Now go back to the first time you remember feeling this way. It may be that

the person in the present context is triggering old traumas. Working on healing the original or core trauma will take the charge off being with this person in the present.

2. Next, relate that trigger to a core value or need that you hold. For example, if you feel triggered when a friend tells another person something you've told them in confidence, the related core value may be that you value trust and confidence in your close relationships. And if you feel triggered when someone shows up at your house without calling first, the core need might be that your personal space and time are respected.

3. Now create an assertive statement that addresses that trigger, and the associated need or value. This statement is firm but not harsh – it comes from a place of love and respect. Here are some examples:

   'I value trust and confidence and the freedom to speak openly with my friends. So I won't share personal thoughts and feelings with you if you continue to pass them on to others.'

   Or: 'I have a need for my personal space and time to be respected. So, much as I love hanging out with you, I need you to call and check before you drop round.'

Or: 'I believe in close and caring relationships – I need you to give me more time and presence than you have until now.'

Initially, you may feel that you have to include apologies or disclaimers within these statements. Resist the urge – remember that you deserve to communicate your needs *and* to request that other people meet them. Equally, the other person is free to communicate their own needs, and you can make it clear that you'll listen if and when they decide to do that. Setting boundaries in this way gets easier the more you do it.

4. Communicate your assertive statement to the person concerned with a calm, clear mind. Avoid throwing it out there in the middle of an argument or when you're already feeling triggered. It's great to speak your boundaries in person, in a peaceful moment, but if that feels too difficult, you can put them in a message too.
5. Stick to the boundaries you've set. If you've known the person concerned for a long time and have never built healthy boundaries before, initially, they may test them. This is frustrating but completely normal – and it gives you the opportunity to make it clear that you're serious – you don't want your needs to be neglected any longer, and overstepping your boundaries comes with a consequence.

Follow through. For example, if you've said you need them to call you before visiting you at home but they show up unannounced anyway, you can open the door and politely tell them you're busy and will have to see them another day. They might react negatively to begin with. And that's OK. Remember that their reaction is *theirs* to manage; it's not your responsibility. Your responsibility is to communicate your boundaries clearly to other people and continue upholding them even when others overstep them. When you keep on showing respect for the limits you've set, eventually the people around you will realize that they've got to match that respect.

6. Practice! Stay calm, take deep breaths, and keep going.

Make sure your trauma stops with you

When we're unable to heal from traumatic experiences and events, we're not the only ones to suffer. Intergenerational trauma, sometimes called transgenerational trauma or simply generational trauma, is a psychological theory that describes how trauma can be transferred through generations of a family or community.

Bridging the gap between neuroscience and psychodynamic concepts, psychologist Mark Wolynn writes about the personal, neurological, shared, and interactive processes that allow our parents to transmit their trauma to us, or allow *us* to transmit our trauma to our own children.[16] Wolynn, along with other psychology scholars, suggests that if no one 'breaks the cycle,' trauma can be passed along through multiple generations.

The best-known example of this on a large scale is the lasting effects of the Holocaust on Jewish communities, which, to varying degrees, integrated incredible trauma into their way of life and perception of the world. The Satmar community in New York, for example, is an Orthodox Jewish community in which having children is vitally important – to make up for the lives that were taken by the Nazis.[17]

It is, of course, completely understandable that such a horrific experience would stay with a community long after the event, and their trauma can never – and should never – be forgotten. It's impossible for an outsider to judge, but I can't help but hope that all humans will be able, at some point, to put down the weight of the past and live with inner freedom.

And on a smaller scale, trauma is passed through families. All the time. The things your parents didn't heal from have had an impact

---

16 Wolynn, M. (2017), *It Didn't Start with You: How Inherited Family Trauma Shapes Who We Are and How to End the Cycle*. Penguin Books.

17 Kranzler, G. (1995), *Hasidic Williamsburg: A Contemporary American Hasidic Community*. Jason Aronson, Inc.

on your perception of the world. The things your grandparents didn't heal from had an impact on how your parents chose to live. And the things that you don't heal from could have an impact on how your children, or your nieces and nephews, understand their place in life.

When we carry our trauma with us it's almost impossible not to share it – even if we try to hide it and pretend it was never there. Because that hiding, that suppression, is in itself an expression of trauma that can be transferred to other people.

For example, the way that parents interact with their children on a day-to-day level, and deal with certain behaviors, is often based on the way they were raised. In my own community, it was the norm for children to be compared to other kids from a very young age – academically, physically, emotionally, and so on. If we didn't get the grades other kids got, we were deemed failures. Light-skinned babies were considered more beautiful than those with darker skin, and no secret was made of that. We were judged by how we measured up to our peers. But this goes far beyond just my culture...

Navigating comparison culture

Comparison is an issue across the board, and it affects us in powerful ways. Not all of these are negative – neuroscientists such as Dr. Gayannée Kedia and her colleagues have described how comparison is a part of the natural brain mechanisms that function to drive self-improvement.[18] However, comparing people, especially children, with others also fosters insecurity and makes it difficult for them to accept themselves.

We all compare our accomplishments, looks, skills, grades, intelligence, popularity, wealth, relationships, and so on with those of others, and use other people as a way to evaluate ourselves. The way we're socialized creates a system of being judged within all social contexts, ranging from the family to educational settings, community groups, friends, work situations, and so on. Because *we* were judged, we become our biggest inner critic; and we also learn to judge others against the same benchmarks we judge ourselves.

With the rise of social media platforms like Instagram, we can now effortlessly access visual stories of people's lives, observing some of their greatest captures and moments, including achievements and picture-perfect scenarios. So it's easier than ever to fall into the trap of comparing yourself or your life with someone else's, and to compare other people with the popular ideas and social movements being shared across social media.

18 Kedia, G., et al. (2014), 'Brain mechanisms of social comparison and their influence on the reward system': www.ncbi.nlm.nih.gov/pmc/articles/PMC4222713 [Accessed January 2, 2021]

We have this instant and constantly accessible framework into which we want to fit everyone. It plays to the very human desire to categorize and make sense of everything; if we're not sure what *we*, personally, think of someone (or ourselves), we just go online and see what boxes they currently do or don't fit into.

We can use our tendency to compare ourselves to others to inspire and motivate us, and having aspirations isn't a bad thing. But if we haven't learnt how to be discerning, and analyzed our thoughts and where they come from using mindfulness and awareness, comparison can *hurt* us. It kills our joy and it can be the dangerous seed that grows into poor mental health.

A strong comparison culture can be a form of generational trauma that's passed down from adults to children, again and again. It becomes so normal to us that we don't even know it's dangerous. We don't notice that it's having an impact on what we think of ourselves and others. We don't understand that it's creating judgment and pain.

Because after all, how can something that so *many* of the parents around us do to their kids – a common, socially acceptable parenting technique – be bad? The same goes for shaming children as a way to stop certain behaviors, or isolating them from connection and social contact when they've done something we don't like. All normal; and all potentially very harmful.

When we carry our trauma with us it's almost impossible not to share it – even if we try to hide it and pretend it was never there. Because that hiding, that suppression, is in itself an expression of trauma that can be transferred to other people.

How can you tell if comparison has become a norm in your life? Here are some of its most common effects:

- A lack of self-worth or a sense of unworthiness.
- Poor self-esteem and low self-confidence.
- The illusion of underachievement.
- Dissatisfaction.
- Validating our existence based on how we compare to others.
- Being judgmental toward others.
- Persistent negative emotions such as envy, hate, guilt, remorse, and jealousy.
- Lying (pretending to be something you're not).
- Disordered eating.

When comparison isn't coupled with very strong self-awareness, it has two basic outcomes: thinking you're not good enough, or thinking you're superior to others.

If you carry family or community trauma with you – or if you've personally been through trauma in your life – it *can* stop with you.

Even if you can't uncover all the secrets of the past or solve every single riddle, you can work on your inner experience, and on your outer expression of trauma, whether it's firsthand, secondhand, or passed down to you from many generations ago. You're doing the work to reimagine your impressions and expressions.

In the next chapter, we'll go deeper into this by exploring the practice of 'reparenting' yourself. You'll learn to build new beliefs (positive, liberating, empowering ones) by responding to yourself with the same love, curiosity, and honesty that you'd give to a child.

But before we get there, I'd like you to work through one more practice in this chapter. It will prepare you for the work we'll do next – as you begin to rewrite the subconscious beliefs you have about yourself and create the conditions you need for genuine inner healing.

Practice #5: Uncover your limiting beliefs

Now that you've written your personal history list (Practice #4, p.118), it's time to meditate on it. This meditation practice is designed to allow you to recognize the limiting beliefs you hold – those that are rooted in the experiences you acknowledged during the list-writing practice.

Essentially, what I'm asking you to do is to sit with your trauma. The big stuff and the small stuff. Sit with it, and notice what stands out. Depending on the length of your list, the practice could take up to an hour, a day, a week, or longer. Feel free to split it into shorter sessions; for example, you could divide your list into smaller lists of 10 memories each, and meditate on *one* of those smaller lists at a time.

Whether you decide to do it all at once or take it slowly, make sure you get to the end of your list. It's important to sit with *all* of it. It's absolutely, perfectly OK for this to take some time. Inner healing isn't a quick-fire, snappy process; we're in this for true, deep, sustainable results. If you need to move slowly, give yourself permission to do so – you can work at a pace that feels right for you.

And again, this practice might feel really uncomfortable. The stuff on your list is messy; some of it may be painful, and some of it may be things that you've worked really hard, for years and years, to forget. We're reshaping beliefs here – rewriting the pages that lay out who you are (or at least, who you think you are). That's never going to be a totally comfortable process.

We can use our tendency to compare ourselves to others to inspire and motivate us, and having aspirations isn't a bad thing. But if we haven't learnt how to be discerning, and analyzed our thoughts and where they come from using mindfulness and awareness, comparison can *hurt* us.

Bring to light

Find a safe, comfortable space. Ideally, you'll know that no one's going to rush in and interrupt you.

1. Settle into a seated position. You can choose to sit on the floor or on a chair; your posture isn't too important here, so just make sure you feel comfortable.

   If you're on the floor, sit on a cushion or two so that your hips are higher than your knees. Feel free to sit with your back against a wall if that helps you feel supported. If you opt to sit on a chair, make sure that the edge of the seat just touches the back of your knees, and that both of your feet are resting firmly on the ground. Have a glass of water or a cup of herbal tea by your side (but nothing containing caffeine because that can heighten anxiety, which is unhelpful when you're working through challenging memories).

2. Place your personal history list in front of you – somewhere you can see it easily. Either your full list, or that shorter, split list if you've decided to work through this practice in smaller sessions. And have your pen there too, with a blank page of your notebook open. Title the page 'Limiting beliefs.'

3. Close your eyes. Allow your hands to rest comfortably on your legs – wherever they naturally fall. Take a deep breath in through the nose and sigh it out through the mouth – releasing all of the air

from your body. Do this twice more – inhaling through the nose, exhaling through the mouth.

4. Allow the breath to return to a natural rhythm. No need to control it. Just notice it. You're arriving in this moment. Sit with the breath in this way for as long as you need to – until you feel calm and present. If you've opened your eyes to read this step, gently close them again as you sit and notice the breath.

5. Now open your eyes and focus on the first memory on your list. Number 1. Read it slowly and take it in. And then close your eyes.

6. Hold this memory in your mind. If you feel called to move your hands, please do so – sometimes we feel a desire to place a hand over the heart, or the abdomen, or some other part of the body that feels somehow connected to, or affected by, a particular memory. There's no need to resist that. Allow it to happen. We're working with the whole body, and so we must listen to the whole body. No sensation or emotion needs to be suppressed. Let it come.

7. Spend as much time as you need to with this memory. Notice how it feels in your mind, in your emotional state, and in your body. And when you're ready, ask yourself: *Have I created a belief because of this memory?*

8. If a belief does come to mind, open your eyes briefly and *write it down in your notebook*, on the page titled 'Limiting beliefs.' If this doesn't

quite make sense to you yet, here's an example from my own list. I'll talk more about this in the next chapter, but here's the short version:

~ *Memory*: Going hungry as a child when my mother didn't have the money to buy enough food.

~ *Limiting belief*: When food *is* available, I have to eat as much as possible, or binge, because food might not be available tomorrow, or the next day, or the next.

9. Then, when you're ready, move on to the next memory on your list. Work through each memory in turn. Some of them may take longer than others – you might close your eyes to hold a particular memory in your mind and find that actually, it doesn't feel very important after all. You haven't attached any specific belief to it. And so you can let it go and move on quickly.

   And then another memory might feel *huge* – it could take more time than you expect to sit with it and get familiar with what it really means to you, and how it feels. As I said, *give yourself that time*. There's no rush. You're not working to anyone else's schedule. This is all about *your* healing and *your* wellbeing.

10. Sip water. Sip herbal tea. If you feel overwhelmed, return to your breath – just noticing it. Remember where you are. In this body. In this room. In this building. On this Earth. In this Universe. Carry on when you feel ready.

11. When you've worked right through the last memory on your list, take a few moments with your breath. Take three deep breaths in through the nose and exhale through the mouth.

    - This is releasing.
    - You're releasing.
    - You're released.

You've done it. By meditating through your list, you've released memories that you no longer need to hold on to. And you've built a new list – a list of your limiting beliefs. Beliefs you've carried with you throughout your life. Some of them have been with you since you were very young.

I can't tell you how powerful it is, this list in front of you. I know it's been a lot of work to get here; I know it hasn't felt magical or lovely. It's not magic – it really is work. But now you have a list of the limiting beliefs that you've identified. They've been governing how you live your life. You've brought them out of the shadows, into the light of day (or into the light of your lamp, or whatever light you've got going on). You can see them clearly.

What happens when you can see your limiting beliefs clearly like this? You get to change them.

CHAPTER 5

Work with *you* in a new way

The mind is flexible. It wants to learn, and it's willing to change.

Hold on a sec. Can we take a breath together? Just one deep breath, right now.

Because we've been through a lot.

You've been through a lot.

You've been through a lot in your life, and you've been through a lot by moving through this book so far.

How do you feel? If you feel unsettled or unsteady, don't worry. It's normal. Confronting memories, especially the most traumatic ones, and sitting with them, is a big deal. Remember to give yourself time and space to feel good during this process.

What makes you feel good? Perhaps it's going for a walk in nature. Having a coffee with a friend. Spending an evening in with a loved one. Going to the cinema. Cuddling your dog.

You deserve to do the things that lift your spirits and soothe your soul – this healing process doesn't have to be *all* hard. Life is still a big, beautiful experience to be lived! You're still a miraculous arrangement of atoms, a unique expression of energy, and you're *meant* to be here.

The impact of childhood events

We've done a lot of work on accessing experiences and memories, and shedding light on them so we can begin to let them go. In this chapter, we start a new phase in the healing journey – coming to the present moment and looking into the future.

Before we get into that, though, I want to go a little deeper into a concept I touched on earlier: 'reparenting.' Because this is the perfect moment in your journey to take control of the way you want to learn for the rest of your life; to welcome your childlike curiosity and willingness to learn; and to discover how to *choose* the way you respond to things, instead of reacting from earlier impressions or trauma.

Something I've always found fascinating is the way people choose to make themselves unhappy. I'm using the word 'choose' because often, it *is* a voluntary decision. Many of us, including me, participate in experiences that we know are going to cause us pain.

I used to eat for the sake of eating. I'd binge on junk foods – things I could easily access in large quantities. Foods that would make me feel pretty icky, and uncomfortable, and emotionally drained or low. Initially, I thought I did this because I loved food so much, and I was bored. But that reasoning was incomplete.

Eating throughout the day was quite a luxurious activity to appease my boredom, given my tough childhood. When I was young, my family didn't have a lot of money, and there were times when proper meals were scarce. I was used to expecting hunger – I knew that having a solid meal one day didn't necessarily mean I'd have one the next. On top of that, my mother would insist that if I wanted to be strong and healthy, I'd need to eat all my food. This might not seem so tragic – in fact, you could argue that it's normal for parents to tell their kids this – but in the circumstances in which we were raised, I felt great pressure to finish all my food at every opportunity, even if my body was resisting it.

You see, I had a desire to be strong and healthy so I could protect my family from the shady creatures who lurked around our neighborhood (such as kidnappers) or followed us home (such as alcoholics); and from the anonymous strangers who'd call us in the middle of the night and threaten to take away my mum; and from our rowdy and racist neighbors who'd get wasted and disturb us throughout the night.

I feared for my survival and for my family's survival. If food was going to help me protect *them* by making *me* strong and healthy, I was going to keep eating it. Eventually, overeating became habitual.

So, with introspection as I moved through my healing process in recent years, I realized this was the root of my excessive 'boredom' eating. I'd integrated that belief into my way of being – the belief that when food was available, I had to consume as much of it as I could because I'd no idea if I was going to get another meal. It was a response driven by fear and an instinct for survival that had settled deep into my psyche while I was still a developing child. But the outcome in real terms was excess weight, lethargy, and disappointment in myself.

Many of us will do something for the sake of doing it – even if it's unhealthy or it doesn't improve our state of being in any way – and without questioning the *reason* behind it. For example, a woman I worked with a few years back described to me her addiction to her ex. He was a covert narcissist who physically abused her on a regular

You deserve to do the things that lift your spirits and soothe your soul – this healing process doesn't have to be *all* hard. Life is still a big, beautiful experience to be lived! You're still a miraculous arrangement of atoms, a unique expression of energy, and you're *meant* to be here.

basis, yet while it pained her to be with him, she felt empty and bored when she was *not* exposed to his aggression and manipulation. She was disgusted with herself for feeling this way, and for going back to him again and again, but she struggled to break the cycle.

It turned out that as a child she'd lived with abusive caregivers, and that trauma had shaped her view of the world, her relationships, and her need for intense emotional experiences. She associated the trauma with a negative belief about herself; this is very common and it becomes part of why the experience gets stuck and replayed.

And she craved the intensity of abuse – it was like a drug that she'd been programmed to need, even as it destroyed her, bit by bit. Uncertainty made her feel alive. So it was no wonder she kept going back to this man; paradoxically, he was the route to her survival. Her limiting belief, in this case, was that violence and aggression were a necessary part of a relationship. And without it, life couldn't feel... *alive*.

Perhaps, through the work we've done already, you've identified traumatic memories and limiting beliefs that are having an impact on your life today. Have you begun to uncover the reasons behind some of your negative patterns, or the habits you can't shake that you're perpetually frustrated by?

Our limiting beliefs aren't always as obvious as this. Sometimes, a much more subtle event will trigger a belief that will hold us back for years to come. For example, a good friend of mine remembers a moment during his childhood when he was asked a scientific question. He thought he knew the answer, so he said, 'I know! It's...' and relayed what he thought was the answer to the question. The adult who'd posed the question laughed at him openly. 'Nice try,' he said, 'but you're *so* wrong. Don't answer a question like that unless you're sure you know the answer – just say you don't know.'

And as a result of that brief and seemingly insignificant childhood interaction, my friend has spent his entire life *not* stepping up to answer questions. He keeps quiet. He holds the belief that if his response to a question isn't 100 percent accurate, he'll be laughed at and mocked. He's one of the most intelligent guys I know, and thoughtful with it – people would do well to hear his opinions, and I know from our relaxed one-to-one conversations that he brings a lot of insight to any discussion – and yet he holds back, listening to everyone else speak and keeping his own knowledge and opinions to himself.

The power of reparenting

In all of the examples I've given – and in any experience that *you've* had of integrating a limiting belief into your worldview as a child – a process called reparenting could be beneficial.

Our minds have been conditioned by the events we've lived through and the people we've listened to – we've learnt that these can create deep impressions on us. Some of these impressions are positive and helpful, but others are certainly not, and the unhelpful ones create patterns of thought, emotion, and behavior that hold us back. They don't empower us or help us find joy; instead, we experience fear, insecurity, and sadness. And so we suffer.

You aren't responsible for your childhood conditioning, but you need to take responsibility for changing it *now*, as an adult. Blaming your past for a limiting mindset doesn't fix it. You have to seek new ways of thinking and being, and practice those new ways until they become more real to you than your old beliefs.

Practice really is key; and reparenting is a simple tool that you can use every single day. Reparenting is usually taught to parents because it's a way to care for yourself as an adult at the same time as caring for your children, and to address your childhood trauma so you don't pass it on to your kids. But I believe this process can be of value to everyone – parents or not.

Dr. Art Martin, author of the book *ReParenting Yourself*, writes in detail about how we can identify the rejection we experienced as children that now affects the way we react to certain situations as an adult.[19] And in *The Inner Child Workbook*, recovery therapist Cathryn Taylor teaches similar techniques; she guides readers to reparent the child within in order to heal long-lasting shame, anger, and fear of abandonment.

Taylor names six steps for the reparenting process, beginning with identifying pain and figuring out what childhood experience it might come from, then *feeling* the pain, detaching from it, and eventually releasing it to reclaim a childlike sense of joy.[20] I'd recommend both of these books if the idea of reparenting your hurt 'inner child' resonates with you. But here, I'll share my own take on reparenting, which has been influenced by Taylor, Martin, and the other thinkers who've guided me on my healing path.

---

19 Martin, A. (2009), *RePorenting Yourself: Growing up Again; Recovering Your Lost Self*. Personal Transformation Press.

20 Taylor, C. (1991), *The Inner Child Workbook: What to do with your past when it just won't go away*. Jeremy P. Tarcher/Putnam.

For me, reparenting is essentially about reshaping our capacity for learning. It's about welcoming new experiences and making *choices* about what we integrate into our belief system about ourselves and our lives, and what we accept and let go as 'just an experience.'

All experiences – good and bad – have something to teach us. But not all experiences are worth weaving into our understanding of who we are and what we want. The impressions we picked up throughout our childhood have created beliefs that block us from creating *new*, more helpful beliefs. They keep us stuck.

We can all benefit from reparenting

Imagine sitting down with yourself as a child. You're an adult, and you look your childhood self in the eye. You know what this child has learnt. You know what's going to hurt them and hold them back as they grow older. And you get to say, 'Hey, that thing you learnt? It's not true. I completely get why you believe it so deeply, and I know that letting it go might feel hard. And it's OK if you need to cry or shout or scream about it. But it's not true. What *is* true is that you deserve love, and to know that you're safe, and that you're good.'

Blaming your past for a limiting mindset doesn't fix it. You have to seek new ways of thinking and being, and practice those new ways until they become more real to you than your old beliefs.

Sometimes, reparenting is as simple as repeating a childhood interaction in a different way. Remember my friend who keeps his opinions to himself because an adult once mocked him for getting something wrong? He could imagine himself on that day, as a child, and *he* could be the adult. Instead of laughing and embarrassing that child version of himself, he could do what the adult should have done. He could say, 'That's a great answer! Actually, the answer is *this*, but I understand what you're saying, and it's really cool that you know that stuff.'

Two sentences worded differently could change my friend's feelings about sharing his ideas and getting things wrong. This is, of course, reparenting simplified – but that simplicity is powerful in itself. You can do this. You can look at your list of limiting beliefs, go back to the memories attached to them, and be the adult who talks to your childhood self in those moments. What would you do differently? How did your childhood self really need to be treated or spoken to?

This isn't just speculation. Reparenting has been found to be an effective therapeutic process for severely traumatized children and adults,[21] and reparenting techniques are backed up by

21 Willison, B. and Masson, R. (1990), 'Therapeutic Reparenting for the Developmentally Deprived Student': www.jstor.org/stable/23901240 [Accessed January 2, 2021]

neuroscience. Brain-imaging studies show that the adult brain still has the plasticity of a child's brain, although to a lesser degree. What this means is that we still have the capacity to create new neural pathways, or connections, in our brain. Neural pathways are the links between one part of the nervous system and another; they have 'plasticity,' which means they can change (becoming stronger, weaker, disappearing, *or* developing entirely new ones) depending on the experiences, thoughts, and emotions that we have.[22]

For example, if you regularly tell yourself you're worthless when you make mistakes, you may create neural pathways that make that reaction – and the emotions and physical sensations that come with it – more and more automatic. It becomes easier and quicker for you to feel that you're worthless.

But if you change that, and begin to work on telling yourself that you're learning and developing every time you make a mistake, you start to build (and then strengthen) a pathway toward that feeling of growth. The responses you repeat become more and more natural to you, until you jump straight to those responses without even having to think about it.

---

22 Sharma, N., et al. (2013) 'Neural plasticity and its contribution to functional recovery': www.ncbi.nlm.nih.gov/pmc/articles/PMC4880010 [Accessed January 2, 2021]

The new systems of understanding that we create through reparenting can weaken the negative connections we made as children, and build stronger, alternative pathways that give us a more positive way of seeing things.[23] These new pathways are based on our insight and knowledge as adults, rather than on the false beliefs we absorbed from the (inevitably flawed) adults who cared for us when we were young.

Oh, and by the way – by getting this far into this book, you've already begun to reparent yourself – because reparenting is, essentially, the practice of relearning how to acknowledge and meet your needs as an adult. Take a moment to thank yourself for that.

Working through the practice of relearning your needs doesn't mean you had bad parents, or that your parents didn't love you. It just means that your parents were, as all humans are, imperfect; their care for you was influenced by their own limitations, beliefs, and past experiences. They may have done the very best they could with what they had at the time – and it's not an insult to them when you take action to give yourself the care and love you've always needed.

Now let's get into our next practice.

---

23 Lee, A. (2018), 'The Mirror Exercise and the Restructuring of the Parent-Child Relational Unit': www.tandfonline.com/doi/abs/10.1080/03621537.2018.1505117 [Accessed June 28, 2020]

Practice #6: Rewrite your limiting beliefs

In the last chapter you built a list of the limiting beliefs that you've carried with you in your subconscious for some time – perhaps for most of your life (Practice #5). Some of these beliefs will have grown out of specific traumatic or painful experiences. Now is the time to rewrite them. And I mean that quite literally.

Go back to your list of limiting beliefs, and select five memories. Once these memories lose their emotional charge – meaning you can think of the event without the same intensity – add another three memories and continue down your list at a pace that you are comfortable with. Choose the beliefs that are most present in your life – those that dictate your decisions, your relationships, and the way you live in the world. Choose the beliefs that cause you the most doubt and hold you back from taking the risks you wish you were brave enough to take, or that act as barriers between you and the open, powerfully loving relationships you'd like to have.

Maybe they're the beliefs you spent the most time on as you were meditating through your list of memories – because they feel the strongest. As an example, here are some of my own limiting beliefs that I've made a great effort to rewrite using this practice:

- I have no power over my future because my destiny has already been chosen for it – and it looks like a struggle.
- I'll always be financially poor.
- I'll never find true love in this lifetime.
- I've no natural talents or special skills like other people do.
- No one will take my thoughts and opinions seriously if I share them.

You can get started in your own time. Although you can fit this practice into your life at any time of day that works for your schedule, if possible, it's helpful to work through it just before falling asleep or immediately after waking. Neuroscience suggests that the mind is more easily programmable during those moments; this could be because the *theta* brain waves that we experience as we shift from waking to sleeping, or from sleeping to waking, play a key role in our memory and cognitive function.[24]

This state of mind has now been recorded and analyzed in modern brain-imaging studies; however, it's been known for much longer as

24 Zhang, H. and Jacobs, J. (2015), 'Traveling Theta Waves in the Human Hippocampus': www.jneurosci.org/content/35/36/12477 [Accessed May 14, 2020]

an important opportunity to influence the subconscious. Tibetan Buddhists, for example, call this in-between state the 'bardo of dreams,' and have utilized it for centuries as an important time for meditative practices and a preparation for lucid dreaming.[25] So, if you can rewrite your beliefs during that period of subconscious openness, the impact could be stronger or happen more quickly.

Rewrite in the light

Grab your notebook and pen and a hot drink, and settle in.

1. Write down your chosen limiting beliefs in your notebook. I suggest using a blank double page and writing them on the left-hand side.

2. Read through each belief again. As you do so, ask yourself these questions:

    ~ Why have I held on to this belief for so long?

    ~ Does it add any value to my lived experience?

    ~ What would happen if I didn't believe this?

25 Cuevas, B.J. (2003), *The Hidden History of the Tibetan Book of the Dead*. Oxford University Press USA, p.49.

3. Then, on the right-hand page of your notebook, you can rewrite each belief in a *new* way – so they're no longer limiting, and instead become powerful reminders of your potential for growth and freedom. Once you've written them down, they begin to contribute to your vibration, taking you from the low level of limitation to the high, vibrant level of hope and healing.

   As an example, here are those limiting beliefs of my own that I shared earlier, now rewritten into new, empowering beliefs:

   ~ I have the power of choice, and the ability to learn and grow. So I can shape my future.

   ~ I have everything I need to create a fulfilling and successful career and earn the money I need to support the lifestyle I want to have.

   ~ I'm capable of love, and I'm worthy of being loved. I have the capacity to build a strong relationship grounded in true love.

   ~ My experience and inner self are unique, and I'm free to nurture my talents and discover how to make the greatest impact I can in this life.

   ~ My thoughts and opinions are valuable and I have the confidence to share them.

4. Begin to focus your whole self on your new beliefs. To do this, you'll need to start building a body of evidence for *why* these new beliefs can be true for you. Think through the following questions, and then write down your answers on a new page in your notebook:

    - What has happened in my life so far that supports this new belief?
    - What can I do *today* to act in line with this new belief?
    - How would I behave, move, communicate, and feel if this belief were my deepest truth?

5. This final step is an ongoing one. Because from now on, you'll need to bring your newly written beliefs to mind on a regular basis. Maybe even every day. There are a number of ways to reinforce positive replacement beliefs, including writing them down on sticky notes and putting them behind your wardrobe door, on the car dashboard, the fridge, the bathroom mirror, and so on. You can also set alarms on your phone and set the phrases as reminder messages. Whenever you find yourself feeling an emotion in response to one of your limiting beliefs – or taking action or making a decision because of it – pull out the new belief and consider how and what *that* inspires you to feel, act, or choose.

Your newly rewritten beliefs will do several things:

- Act as a simple way to reparent yourself – some of your rewritten beliefs might be the things you wish the adults in your life had told you about yourself when you were young. You can begin telling yourself these things now, and integrate them into your subconscious just as deeply as the limiting beliefs you created early in life. *You* are the adult now; and this wisdom is emanating from the steps you are clearly taking to review and reflect on your life, which is not something that most people do.

- Help you flip your perspective every time you notice that you're acting, or reacting, in a way that's grounded in your old subconscious beliefs. When you feel yourself spiraling into an old pattern, you can take out your rewritten beliefs and use them as a tool to get you back onto your healing path.

- Spark a new relationship with learning. In terms of the seven bodies, we're working with the mental body here, and this exercise activates your capacity for a kind of intellectual, academic study of the self. That capacity, when it's in full flow, will keep you curious and be a positive driving force on your ongoing inner healing journey.

With my own rewritten beliefs, initially I had to make a conscious effort to remind myself of them every single day. But over time they've become more natural – the more I access them, the stronger the neural pathways that led me to them have become, and so it's easier and easier for me to truly believe them.

The curiosity cure

Do you ever feel like you're not learning anything? Or even deeper than that, do you feel as if you're not *interested* in learning anything?

This is a response to fear or trauma. It's a response to being hurt.

It doesn't always happen. And actually, immediately after a difficult event, you may well experience the opposite for a short period of time. You may get a burst of energy – something bad has happened and you want to rebuild yourself quickly and productively by filling your life with new things, new ideas, new people, new skills.

Getting a new hairstyle after a breakup is a classic example of this; or booking an adventurous trip just after we go through some kind of life-changing grief; or moving to a new city or country when we feel overwhelming rejection from our family. But then... the reality of our emotions sets in. And a much longer-lasting trauma response takes over.

While we're afraid or hurting, we want to stay safe. Everything in the body and brain is programmed to force us to protect ourselves, and sticking with what we know is – as far as our primal systems are concerned – a pretty sure way of avoiding danger. Because the unknown is dangerous, right?

So, we hunker down. We shuffle inward. Not in a reflective, contemplative way, but as a means of retreat. That might show up in our life as a reluctance to go out and about, or socialize, or make an effort with our appearance, or take good care of our body. But all of those things go hand in hand with the shutting down of curiosity and connection.

I'd like to put the record straight – curiosity didn't kill the cat. Curiosity trained the cat's muscles, honed its hunting skills, and got the cat its next meal.

When our emotional wounds kill our curiosity we lose a bit of the life in us. We become dull – not just to other people, but to ourselves. Everything feels less interesting. Less exciting. Less worth getting up for in the morning. It's a completely understandable reaction. Why would you remain engaged with a world that you know is so full of threat and the potential for pain? Why wouldn't you batten down the hatches and shut it all out?

But as scary as it might feel to step out into the world with a willingness to absorb anything that comes your way, social connection is essential for healing. When you approach your inner healing journey with that willingness – some days, it might even feel like a kind of *playfulness* – you can do the following:

- Open new doors. Even the ones that feel scary can be worth opening; if you're willing to find out what's on the other side, you can create a whole new world of potential to be pleasantly surprised.
- Find a new sense of acceptance of your own emotions and experiences. Instead of thinking, *I hate it that I feel this way!* try, *It's interesting that I feel this way. I wonder what else I'll find in there if I spend a bit of time with these feelings and look deeper.*
- Learn. Learn about yourself and learn about other people; learn new ways of seeing things; learn new ways of reacting to things; learn new ways of interacting with others; learn about things that interest you (even if they've nothing in particular to do with healing – just because learning is a joyful act); learn how to care for yourself; learn how to give love and receive love without fear… just learn.

- Let go of judgment. If you're curious, you know there's always more than one perspective. So, judging yourself or others for emotions or reactions clearly becomes counterproductive; you become a scientist of the self, instead of a critic.

- Meet exciting people. Curiosity instantly lifts you up and connects you with all the infinite potential out there. People who are vibrating low and heavy aren't curious. But people who are vibrating high, vibrant, alive with energy? Always curious. *Always.*

Trusting the process

Do you remember what curiosity felt like when you were really young? Maybe it's hard to recall. But give it a minute. You wanted to know anything and everything. You asked 'why?' so often that the adults around you rolled their eyes in frustration.

What if you could approach your own inner healing work with that same open mind? What if you could become curious about your ability to be your own healer?

Explore that. Ask questions. If you feel able to, talk with other people about recovering from difficult experiences, and mending emotional wounds, and moving forward in life with a new approach.

Reconnect with curiosity. Find ways to ask the questions *why?* and *how?* Welcome the myriad of answers you receive. Study yourself, but always with kindness and a conscious effort not to judge. Become your own observer. You're here to do big things, even if it doesn't seem like it right now.

But let's be clear about this: I'm not asking you to throw out everything that you currently use to define yourself. I'm not asking you to become a different person, or to alter your personality completely. I'm definitely not asking you to become a mala bead-wearing caricature of a 'healer,' who allows 'good vibes only' in their life and refuses to face any negativity. After all, as I outlined in my first book, what we resist will persist.

I'm inviting you to ask questions. To go inward in a *different* way – not to close yourself off but to open yourself up – to welcome the whole spectrum of emotions that comes with being human, and to embrace the lessons you can find in negative experiences as well as wonderful ones. And this doesn't mean never being scared. Actually, it means being scared quite a lot, because opening ourselves up and deciding to be curious means we can step closer to our vulnerability while making it feel safe to do so – like holding a rope or being securely harnessed while approaching the edge of a cliff. It makes us walk into the unknown, so we can discover what happens out there.

When I offer advice, there are a few phrases I hear often:

- 'That's easier said than done.'
- 'You wouldn't understand.'
- 'It's easy for you to say.'

Let's be honest: I haven't lived the worst imagined life. Also, I haven't been in your shoes. And everything is easier said than done. We can never completely understand others and their path because we're not living their lives. However, just like everyone else, there's a lot I *have* been through. We all face hardships in our lives, even if some are deemed worse than others (or are objectively worse than others).

Some of the things I've experienced, particularly early in my life, could be perceived as pretty devastating. Nevertheless, no matter what you've been through, there's a good chance that you and I have had similar feelings at times. I've wanted to give up on life on numerous occasions – because I've felt that it hasn't been fair, or I've imagined some kind of hidden universal agenda against me. Does this sound familiar to you?

This is why I'm so grateful for my horrific history and cruel lessons. Just imagine if I hadn't been through the tough times and suffered the trauma I did. I'd have nothing inspiring to write about and nothing to serve as a contrast to my happier times – because it's those very contrasts that help bring better times into relief, thereby allowing us to notice and appreciate them. Imagine if I'd had it easy my whole life but still felt called to go out and offer advice and support people in their self-healing work. Would you be able to relate to me? Probably not.

Without hard times and hurt, I wouldn't be able to pass on what I've learnt through my personal healing journey. The way I've dealt with my mental health and my personal problems allows me to guide others as they figure out how to deal with theirs. Those who devote themselves to self-healing will eventually heal others. Even if they don't write a book about it, their presence and wisdom will be transmitted to the people around them.

You have to trust that the process will help you progress. Everything you go through helps you grow – the good, the bad, and everything in between. During tough times, don't be too hard on yourself. If you make the mistake of falling into the role of victim, you'll continue to be treated like one. Simply do your best to keep moving forward.

Practice #7: Meditate in a new state of hope

This is a short and simple meditation to help you ground yourself in this moment of your journey. You've rewritten your limiting beliefs about yourself, so you now have a new set of empowering and uplifting beliefs to begin living by. These will become a central part of your healing work, and you can return to them for years to come. They might change (because *you* will change), and you must always allow those changes to happen. Don't resist it if one of the beliefs you've written no longer speaks to you. Rewrite it again.

This is *your* journey. Let these beliefs become a kind of adaptable, evolving manifesto for your life, giving you strength when you need it, and reminding you in your darkest moments that you're capable of seeing things in a different way.

This meditation will help you integrate your rewritten beliefs into your subconscious mind, and absorb their meaning into your personal vibration. You can practice it once if that's all you feel you need, but if it feels good, do it regularly. And if you do rewrite your beliefs again later on, do this meditation again.

Reintegrate. Remind. Rework.

During tough times, don't be too hard on yourself. If you make the mistake of falling into the role of victim, you'll continue to be treated like one. Simply do your best to keep moving forward.

As it's written, the meditation takes just 10 minutes, but if you'd like to sit with it for longer, please do. I'll say it again (because it's really, really important) – this is *your* journey and *your* healing. You can do it your way, and you don't have to fit yourself into anyone else's expectations or schedule, especially not mine.

The meditation of possibility

Choose a place where you won't be disturbed for at least 10 minutes. Personally, I love to practice this meditation outside. If that's possible for you, find a quiet spot in a garden, park, or other natural space. Trees make for great meditation buddies, as the Buddha found out many years ago.

1. Find your comfortable seated position. Anything that works for you – kneeling; with legs crossed or straight; or with your back supported against a wall or a tree. Choose a posture that doesn't feel like a huge effort. You want to feel relaxed and able to focus on your inner state, rather than constantly shifting around trying to ease discomfort. If you want to sit on a chair or a bench, go for it.

2. You can close your eyes if you feel comfortable doing so, or keep them open and soften the gaze a few feet in front of you. Allow your focus to blur a little. The eyes are relaxed. If it feels best to practice with the eyes closed, read these instructions a couple of times first:

- Breathe. First, three deep breaths in through the nose and out through the mouth.
- Breathe it in and let it out. Then place both hands on your ribcage, with the fingers just touching in the center.
- Breathe into both hands – expanding the front of the ribs. And breathe out.
- Breathe into the right hand – expanding the right side of the ribs. And breathe out.
- Breathe into the back of the ribs – expanding the back of the body. And breathe out.
- Breathe into the left hand – expanding the left side of the ribs. And breathe out.

Repeat this circular breathing pattern once more. Then let your hands rest wherever they fall on your legs. Let go of control of the breath. Observe its natural rhythm. Notice how the body feels.

3. Bring to mind an encompassing statement about your newly rewritten beliefs about yourself. What's their overall message? What are you trying to teach yourself? To give yourself? Perhaps the underlying message – the thread that runs through them all – is that you deserve love, from yourself and others. Maybe it's that

you're strong. Confident. Creative. Capable. Maybe it's that the potential that lies in your future is bright, and big, and brilliant.

Don't think too hard; just allow a statement to drift into your mind; for example:

- 'I'm giving myself permission to love and be loved.'
- 'I'm stepping into my strength and confidence.'
- 'I'm excited for what the future may hold.'

4. Allow a smile to pass across your face. A soft, calm smile. Feel the hope that lies in the work you've already done. The love you've given yourself. The challenges you've already overcome on this journey. And the leaps you've made in becoming your own healer. In stepping into your power in that perfectly unique role that belongs *only* to you.
5. Breathe gently here for a few more moments. Finally, bring the palms of your hands to the lower abdomen. Feel the warmth of the hands radiating inward. The energy you give to yourself. Notice the warm steadiness at the core of your body. Take one more deep breath in through the nose and sigh it out through the mouth.

Your practice is complete. In your own time, open your eyes or refocus your gaze.

CHAPTER 6

Who are you?

Your true Self may be obscured by layers of experience and expectation, but you can always return to being truly you.

People talk a lot about 'being yourself.'

'Just be yourself,' they say. 'Don't try to be someone else – just be you.'

Or, in more spiritual communities, you might hear something like: 'Reconnect with your true nature.' I won't lie, I've definitely said something like this at some point, and I'll definitely say it again later in this chapter.

But if you don't really know who you are, then those statements are meaningless. What does it *mean* to be yourself? What *is* your true nature? And how do you find out?

I prefer to ask the question like this: Who would you be, how would you feel, and what would you do if you'd never been hurt? If nobody else existed, or had ever shared their opinion about you.

I know – *that's* not an easy question either. But at least it's more specific – it gives us something to work with. The implication is that who you really are is you without the pain and fear. You without the wounds. You without the trauma.

I don't mean that we need to wipe clean our emotional slate and behave as if everything's blissfully perfect. I firmly believe that our challenges are a part of our strength; the difficult things we go through really do shape who we are, what we feel, and what we do, and there's no getting around that. Even when we fully accept our trauma and feel at peace with everything in our lives up to this moment, we've still adapted. We've gathered information and integrated it. Even our newly rewritten beliefs were inspired by our old limiting beliefs – and those came from our pain.

We'll always be connected to the things that have hurt us, but that doesn't have to be a bad thing. The connection between us and our trauma can become our strength; it can give us empathy, allow us to support others, teach us what we're capable of, and remind us to appreciate the crystalline beauty in mundane moments because we know how bad things can be. We know that this moment is good because we've lived through terrible ones.

Who would you be, how would
you feel, and what would you
do if you'd never been hurt?
If nobody else existed, or had ever
shared their opinion about you.

Instead, considering who you'd be if you'd never been hurt is about getting to know your innate energy. Your vibration is bashed about by your experiences, relationships, interactions, and impressions, but there's a steady hum of complete 'youness' somewhere in there. And no matter what's going on, or what stage of hurt or healing you're at, that steady hum is always there. Think of it as your natural equilibrium.

And equilibrium is something that can always be returned to, if we do the work to rebalance what's become out of balance. Part of that work is using what you've already done and taking control of your right to respond – to anything – in the way that *you* want to, rather than the way your trauma wants you to react.

Take control of your right to choose your response

We know that trauma lies. When emotional pain and fear have settled into us, we develop defense mechanisms to keep us safe. Our reactions to triggers are a huge part of that, and perhaps the part that's most visible from the outside.

So, as we teach ourselves to heal ourselves, we have to begin making choices. Instead of reacting instantly when we feel triggered by something or someone, we pause. We thank the person or thing that's triggered us – because they've highlighted a part of us we need to heal – and then choose to respond in the way we really want to respond.

Your rewritten beliefs are useful here. When you feel overwhelmed, and sense that you're about to react to something based on an old pattern or limiting understanding of yourself, shift into the new beliefs. Remind yourself of how you've changed your perspective before – because if you've done it already, you're definitely capable of doing it again, even in the middle of a stressful moment.

In his book *The Four Agreements*, thought leader and author Don Miguel Ruiz offers a code of conduct based on the spiritual wisdom of the ancient Mexican Toltec people; his second agreement states that we shouldn't take anything personally.[26] Another thing that's easier said than done, I know. However, those who attempt to belittle us reveal more about their own character and perception of the world than ours. Those who want to hurt the world outside of them must contain hurt in their inner world. You can only give what you have – literally and energetically.

---

26 Miguel Ruiz, D. (2018), *The Four Agreements: A Practical Guide to Personal Freedom*, Amber-Allen Publishing, Inc.

Imagine you're scrolling on social media and you come across a picture or a caption that triggers you emotionally. You react to someone else's behavior or words. Your vibration becomes lower as you experience feelings such as anger, envy, insecurity, or disappointment. A painful emotion resurfaces and to defend yourself from this hurt, you use aggressive language and spew out hatred in the comment section – in other words, you appear to 'troll' the social media user who made the post. Your reaction has revealed an unhealed emotional wound.

It's like when someone sees a photo of you and your partner and tells you that you're too ugly for your partner. Although the picture of the two of you has triggered that person, they've also triggered *you* with their comment because they've created doubt in you and made you feel as if you're not good enough. These are beliefs based on fear. Those who feel secure and recognize their own worth would remain unchallenged by this particular opinion.

In the short term, you can set boundaries for yourself to manage your reactions. For example, you can make an agreement with yourself that when you feel triggered, you'll give yourself a certain amount of time to pause, let it sink in, and consider how you truly *want* to respond – rather than reacting in the heat of the moment.

Those who attempt to belittle us reveal more about their own character and perception of the world than ours. Those who want to hurt the world outside of them must contain hurt in their inner world. You can only give what you have – literally and energetically.

At the very least, this will save you the potential embarrassment of becoming an internet troll; and in face-to-face situations, it could prevent real conflict in relationships that are important to you.

Reprogramming the mind

The long-term solution is to do the work you're doing as you travel through these pages. Recondition the mind and learn your new empowering beliefs. More than learn them – *integrate* them into your subconscious. Make them a part of your energetic makeup. Repeat your new beliefs over and over and over again until you strengthen the neural pathways connected to them enough that it becomes easy and natural for you to genuinely *believe* them.

So, each time you feel emotionally triggered, use it as an opportunity to grow. Or more specifically (because I don't know about you, but I much prefer specifics over vague advice), use it as an opportunity to consciously strengthen the neural pathways to your new empowering and healing beliefs.

How do you do this? By pausing. Instead of reacting immediately, ask yourself which of your limiting beliefs is most closely connected to this trigger, and the strong emotional reaction you're experiencing. What's driving you to feel this way? Why do you feel a burning need to lash out, or prove the triggering person wrong? Then remind yourself of the *new* belief that most directly addresses this trigger.

Remember earlier, when I talked about the breakup that sent me into a downward spiral? I mentioned that one of my reactions was a universal anger toward women. It was irrational; one woman had hurt me, and my damaged ego and emotional state translated that into my pain being caused by all women. Now I totally realize how wrong that was – and how unfair to an entire sex. But that's what I felt. It was the defensive reaction I jumped to, and it felt powerful.

It wasn't who I truly am. And it was definitely not who I want to be. But, for a time, it made me react to women in a highly triggered and irrational way. When I met a woman who presented herself very confidently, or who spoke about relationships in an authoritative way, I'd react with disdain (usually not directly to her, but in my own head and/or to other people).

She's manipulative, I'd think. *She's just using her femininity to take advantage of men. She doesn't care about equal relationships – she's just saying that to get what she wants.*

If I distill it down, I suppose my limiting belief there was that all women were out to get me. Or out to get men. And later, as I began to accept my history in a more conscious way and did the work of acknowledging my limiting beliefs, I rewrote it. The new belief became this: I know that I can have caring, really loving relationships with genuine, thoughtful, intelligent, and kind women.

I applied my new belief to friendships as well as my relationship with my wife. And when I came into conflict with a woman and I felt that old belief rising up, I paused – and replaced it. I reminded myself that I could have those caring and loving relationships. That women are not out to get me; that women are human beings, just like me, with their own feelings and thoughts and fears and desires.

It took time. I repeated the process. And each time I did, I strengthened the neural pathway that led me to the new belief. Until I didn't have to remind myself of it anymore – it simply became what I believe. So now when I meet a woman who would once have triggered a strong reaction in me, or when I have a disagreement with my wife or a female friend, I don't think, *Argh, she's a woman so she's manipulative and out to get me. She's dishonest and I can't trust a word she says* – I just deal with the situation as a human being interacting with another human being.

Which, of course, is what I should have done all along, but at the time of that particular relationship and breakup, I didn't have the self-awareness to catch my fear-based reaction before it became part of my belief system.

This is just one of many examples that show how my own healing journey helped me to reconnect with who I really am, instead of being who my trauma was unconsciously driving me to be. And that's what this journey will do for you, too. The more you integrate your rewritten beliefs into your way of being, the stronger those pathways in your brain will become, and the more you will be like you.

You'll stop believing the lies that your pain tells you – because you'll be more certain of yourself and you'll be developing skills that allow you to question things, and be curious, and recognize that there's always another way of seeing something.

The you who's always there

In yoga philosophy, the true Self is always there. It's a steady center that we all have in us. In ancient Indian texts called *The Upanishads* it's called the *Atman*, and it's basically Self with a capital S. The true Self is the part of each of us that's eternally connected with everything else: the Universe, the Divine, the universal consciousness, or however you like to describe 'everythingness.' We all come from the same stuff and go back to the same stuff.

I had a teacher of Advaita Vedanta – a nondualistic school of Hindu philosophy that focuses on self-realization – who described this true Self to me using a story. I don't know where it originated: I expect it's something that's been shared in lots of different ways by many different people. So this is my own version of it, written for you.

Two waves rush toward the shore. The first wave is anxious; he's fretting, and thinking at a hundred miles an hour about what's about to happen. Thoughts like:

When I reach the shore, that's it, I'll break. My life will be over.

I want to slow down and take it in but I can't – my impulse is to move forward. I can't stop myself.

That other wave is bigger than me. I wish I were bigger.

And it's faster than me, too – I'm not good enough.

I'm scared! I don't want this! I want this all to stop!

I want to be a wave for longer – there's so much more to experience!

This stressed-out and panicky wave doesn't enjoy the experience of traveling toward the shore. He can't take in the beauty of it because he's worrying about the end, and about all the things that might go wrong, and about wanting to control or change the situation.

The true Self is the part of each of us that's eternally connected with everything else: the Universe, the Divine, the universal consciousness, or however you like to describe 'everythingness.' We all come from the same stuff and go back to the same stuff.

The second wave, however, is calm. He rushes just as quickly toward the shore – because that's what waves do – but he isn't scared. He thinks thoughts like:

This is a beautiful life.

I'm glad to be a wave for these few moments.

I won't break or die when I hit the shore because I'll simply go back to the ocean.

I came from the ocean and I'll return to it.

It is what I am, and I am what it is.

This is how I'm meant to be.

The second wave is in touch with the steady, peaceful, even blissful (if you'll forgive me for using such a word) true Self at his core. In contrast, the first wave is not; he's distracted by impressions he's picked up since becoming a wave, and panicking about losing his wave status, and so he can't notice or enjoy how great it is just to be a wave for a little while.

You're the wave. The Universe is the ocean. If you're calm and connected with who you really are, you can be peaceful and connected with the energy of the Universe. Your vibration is tuned in with that universal energy. You're not disturbed or hurt by the impressions and experiences you pick up on your way through life because at your core, you know that you're steady, happy, and calm.

That true Self is always there. It's the equilibrium you can always return to.

Practice #8: Acknowledge what you know to be true about you in this moment

Reconnecting with your true nature, or the real *you* that exists, always, at your core, isn't something you can do in an instant. And that sense of being connected and aware of who you really are comes and goes – unless you're a monk who can spend 12+ hours a day meditating in isolation and silence; a practice that for most of us is neither practical nor appealing.

I definitely believe you can reach a place of growth where you always feel the presence of your true Self beneath the surface; you know it's there, constant and steady, and you know how to get back to it. But the impressions and experiences and pressures of everyday life in our busy modern world take us away from that true nature, again and again. So part of our job, as individuals committed to our own healing and growth, is to return to it – again and again.

This is the first of two simple meditation practices you'll work through in this chapter, using awareness and affirmation to ground yourself. They both utilize skills and insight you've gained so far in this book – so don't worry, you're not going in cold. And they both work quickly to bring you first into the present moment and then into the truth at the heart of you.

You do need to practice the first one before you move on to the second one, though, so please resist the temptation to jump ahead. We're playing the slow game here, remember – there aren't any shortcuts to real inner freedom.

And like the other meditation practices I've shared so far, know that you can repeat this one whenever it feels like it could be helpful. It's a good practice to help you stay aware of your progress – the first time you try it, it might be difficult to answer the question within it, but the further you move along on your healing path, the easier it will be to recognize what's true about you.

The present truth meditation

You can use this practice at any time. It's particularly useful for overcoming anxiety or panic in difficult moments because it brings you

right back to the moment and allows you to question – without judging – the thoughts that are present in your mind.

1. Find your comfortable seated position in a place where you won't be disturbed for 10 minutes. You know the drill.

2. Place both hands on your chest. Feel your chest rise and fall as you breathe in an easy, natural rhythm. You can close your eyes if you feel comfortable doing so, or keep them open and the gaze soft. If it feels best to practice with the eyes closed, read these instructions a couple of times over first.

3. Take your awareness to the ground beneath you and to the parts of your body that are connected with the floor (or chair, or cushion, or whatever you're sitting on). Allow yourself to ground through those connections. Your sit bones are steady on the floor/chair. Your spine rises tall, drawing energy up from the Earth.

4. Become aware that you're *here*. In this place. In this moment. Notice any sounds that you can hear outside the room. You don't need to do anything. Just notice. Allow the sounds to be there.

   And then notice any sounds you can hear inside the room. Again, nothing to do – simply notice.

   Notice any sounds you can hear in your own body. Perhaps the soft sound of the breath. Or even subtler sounds.

Use this process of noticing sound to become more aware of where you are. Here. In this moment.

5. And then consider this question: What is true about you in this moment?

   Answer it silently in your mind, and without feeling any pressure to come up with a 'right' answer. Answer it in any way that feels right to you.

   You might start with what you can feel... It's true that you can feel the connection between your body and whatever it is you're sitting on.

   It's true that you're breathing.

   It's true that you're healing.

   And then go further. Make it more personal. It doesn't matter if not all of the things you know to be true about yourself are positive. There's no need to judge any thought that arises as either positive or negative; allow each thought just to *be*.

   But if a negative belief does come up, allow yourself to question it. Why is it true? What if it isn't?

   What do you know to be true about you?

6. When you feel you've answered the question, return your awareness to the breath. Notice your chest rise and fall beneath your hands. Notice how the spine extends very slightly with each inhale, and then relaxes, just a little, with each exhale.

   Now speak the following affirmation, either out loud (if you feel comfortable doing so) or silently in your mind. Remain present and focused on each word, and evoke the full power of your heart, mind, and body to make the affirmation purposeful:

   It's true that I'll move past this moment and enjoy the freedom of my existence in this life.

7. Send warm, kind energy from the palms of your hands into your heart. There's a sense of calm and love in this moment.

That's it. Well done. Let it go.

The future is different

Another of those painful things that fear makes us believe is that our lives can never change. We create trauma narratives for ourselves. *This happened to me, and then that happened, and then this other thing, and so now I'm just waiting for the next terrible thing. This is my life. I can never be happy or peaceful because I know I'm destined for more bad times.*

And it's a self-fulfilling prophecy. If we expect more trauma, we'll look out for it; maybe we'll even seek it out, even if we don't exactly know we're doing it. So we get trapped in a cycle of being hurt and then expecting hurt, and then being hurt and waiting for more. There's not much room for happiness and growth there, right?

One of the easiest places to see this cycle in action is in the relationships we choose. Often, due to the paradox of comfort through pain, incompatible couples cling on to each other. One half of the couple forms their identity around their partner and finds that without their 'other half,' their image of themselves is shattered.

Some people can't recognize who they are or what their life is without having that other person present in their life. Don't get me wrong, that can always change – and if you're screaming 'This is *me*!' you're in a good place for finding your way out of this box. However, the glue that keeps this identity in place is a combination of the memories and imagined potential of that person.

People tend to believe that their illusion of the present is the ultimate truth. They don't realize that they've created it themselves, through the lens of the past and future (or more accurately, their personal perception of the past and future). Their present lens is distorted by two places that exist only as mental constructs. The past and future don't exist in the physical realm, but we travel to them regularly to present ourselves with 'facts' about our current relationship, or to justify our actions and decisions in the present time.

Sure, the past is beneficial when it comes to inspiring a positive shift in our mindset, such as remembering all the great things that a person's done. And yes, any future mental space can be occupied by empowering thoughts to manifest change – for example, through visualization, which we'll get to shortly. Nevertheless, the way a person behaves today, in the present, rather than how they behaved in the past, ultimately defines where they're at on their journey and if they're genuinely committed to your relationship. You'll find answers right in front of you or within you, not behind you or ahead of you.

Past doings and promises aren't a reflection of the present situation, even if they've helped to form it (remember, we've manifested the present based on patterns that stem from the past). Layers of distorted perception will always hide the ultimate truth.

Realizing that you love the *memories* of a person more than the person can be uncomfortable, even painful – because an illusion that's protected and held you is being destroyed. But it's a step toward letting go of unhealthy attachments, and healing. By extension, you'll open yourself up to a better relationship – one that really is based on love and respect, and that has a bright future.

Destroying illusions, as tough as it might be, is your avenue to a greater and more authentic future. Whether it's a relationship pattern, or any other cycle in which trauma seems to be repeated time and time again, this question is always a useful place to start: *What would you do if you'd never been hurt?* If you think that an 'undamaged' version of yourself would make different choices, such as leaving this relationship or this job or this situation or cycle… Well, you probably know what you need to do.

Your current situation doesn't reflect who you really are. Perhaps it's based on the same kind of fear that the first wave felt – fear that this is as good as it's going to get, that you're not good enough, that others are better than you, and that you're rushing at a terrifying pace toward something you don't want to happen. So switch it up. What would the second wave choose?

Practice #9: Acknowledge what you hope can be true about you in the future

This is our first full visualization exercise. I've saved it for this point in the journey because although visualization is practiced by lots of different people in lots of different ways, it's not easy to do it well if you're not already familiar with getting grounded in your body, in yourself, and in the present moment.

But now you're familiar with those things. We've spent time working through the past, and working through the more tangible 'bodies' – from the physical to the mental. And now we can work with more subtle aspects of the self.

Every part of the healing process is transformative and, in my opinion – as someone who's not currently in the trenches of working through painful past memories; I know that's tough – exciting. But beginning to visualize your true Self in the future is possibly the *most* exciting part because there are no limits here. You don't have to color within the lines – you can imagine anything and everything that you truly want, and make it real in your mind, if only for a few minutes.

The magic of this is that although it's not 'real' in an empirical, outside-world sense, your subconscious mind and energetic vibration don't distinguish between the images you create with your mind and the images you absorb from outside.[27] So when you're deep in a 'future true Self visualization,' you create the same energy and subconscious impressions that'd be created if this visualization were actually happening in your 'real' life.

This does two important things:

1. It settles your hopes and desires into your subconscious mind. Deeply. In a way that means you'll begin working toward the elements of your visualization naturally. Something within you begins to believe that this will become real. I wrote more about this concept in my first book, but basically, a shift happens in the way you behave, and the choices you make, and the actions you take. Which makes your dreams for the future all much more likely to become real.

2. Your vibration shifts in line with the energy of that future true Self visualization. The energy you radiate becomes the same energy that you'd radiate if you were there, in the future, living your dream life and being *you* in the way that you most want to be.

---

27 Pearson, J., et al. (2015), 'Mental Imagery: Functional Mechanisms and Clinical Applications': www.ncbi.nlm.nih.gov/pmc/articles/PMC4595480 [Accessed March 16, 2020]

Realizing that you love the *memories* of a person more than the person can be uncomfortable, even painful – because an illusion that's protected and held you is being destroyed. But it's a step toward letting go of unhealthy attachments, and healing.

If, in your visualization practice, you're confident and calm and respected and completely at peace with everything that's happened in your past, then you vibrate on that level. You send out that energy into the Universe. And what you give, you can receive back.

This works on a physical level. As author and researcher Dr. Joe Dispenza writes: 'We don't need to win the race, the lottery, or the promotion before we experience the emotions of those events. Remember, we can create an emotion by thought alone. We can experience joy or gratitude ahead of the environment to such an extent that the body begins to believe that it is already "in" that event. As a result, we can signal our genes to make new proteins to change our bodies to be ahead of the present environment.'[28]

So this practice is a powerful part of our healing process. It taps into the subtleties of the self in a new way; and crucially, you're doing this at a time when you're ready to make the most of it. You've laid the groundwork and your journey is well underway.

---

28 Dispenza, J. (2012), *Breaking the Habit of Being Yourself: How to Lose Your Mind and Create a New One*. Hay House, Inc. p.80.

Dare to hope

This practice can be done in your usual comfortable seated position or you can choose to do it lying down; it's a great one to work through at the end of the day, in bed. You can drift gently into sleep afterward – and allow your visualization to settle even deeper into your subconscious as it leaves its impression on your dreams.

1. Settle into your preferred position. Close your eyes, or keep them open and soften the gaze. If it feels best to practice with the eyes closed, read these instructions a couple of times over first, and then go for it.

   Take a deep breath in and imagine the breath traveling to every cell of your body. Breathing right into the tips of the fingers, and the tips of the toes, and the crown of the head. Hold the breath in for a few seconds and then slowly release it. Allow the breath to return to an easy, natural rhythm. No control. No effort.

2. Remember the body scan we did earlier – the very first practice in the book? Call to mind a similar awareness of the body now. There's no need to notice every part of the body in turn – although if you've time and you'd like to, feel free – but do become aware of the whole body. A complete, perfect, harmonious organism. Everything connected.

You're completely aware of the whole body.

In this place. In this moment. In stillness and in calm.

3. Then bring the awareness to your thoughts. Notice the movement of your mind; thoughts passing through and lingering for a moment, and then passing on. No thought is good or bad. There's no need to judge. Allow each thought to exist, and then release it.

4. Now you can begin to take control of directing your thoughts. Imagine yourself five years from now. Picture it as if you're really there – begin to build an image in your mind; a reality.

    ~ Five years have passed and you've spent that time working in a focused, kind, and purposeful way on your healing journey. You've let go of painful memories and brought suppressed pain to the surface. You've grieved for that pain; grieved for the version of you who'd never processed that pain. And you've accepted it.

    ~ And over these five years, as you've become more and more connected with who you really are, and more and more aware of your limiting beliefs and patterns, you've changed. Or rather, you've returned to equilibrium. You're not a different person – you're the same person but you no longer carry your wounds so rawly.

    ~ Your emotions are no longer heavy.

~ You're free. You're healed.

~ And in this state, your life has begun to change. You've achieved goals you always dreamed of. You've built strong, loving, fulfilling relationships. You feel whole.

~ Visualize yourself standing in this moment, five years from now. As if you're really there.

~ Notice where you are. What you have. How you feel.

~ Make it as detailed as you like; you might notice the clothes you're wearing, the body language you're using, the people around you. And become aware of where you're at in your life – imagine the job you're doing, the home you're living in. Anything that feels important to you.

~ You're not just creating a picture here, more an entire scene. Involve your senses, too. Where are you? What does that place smell like? What objects are you surrounded by, and what do they feel like? What can you hear? Taste?

~ This moment of feeling good, and feeling better, and feeling healed, is *yours*. Embrace the creativity you have within you and conjure it completely. There's no wrong way to do this.

- ~ For example, if you feel that when you've overcome your trauma and fear you'll be able to build the relationship you've always dreamed of, then visualize yourself with that person. They are in the moment with you and you can feel their arm around you, smell their scent, and see the depths of their eyes looking back at you.

- ~ Or if you feel that when you get to that future moment you'll have a certain home, or a certain appearance, or a certain lifestyle, include these things in your scene. There are no limitations here, and no judgment either. Make it yours.

- ~ Be in this moment. Five years from now.

5. You feel whole. Experience it.

   Don't worry if it feels far-fetched to begin with. It doesn't matter. This practice is almost like... trying your future on for size. Feeling into the potential that exists if you commit to your inner healing. Seeing for yourself how worth it this will all be.

6. And then, in your own time, notice the breath again. The rhythm of the breath; the length of the breath, and the depth of the breath.

   Gently and slowly return to the present moment. To your body, right here and now.

Your practice is complete. You've begun to acknowledge what your true Self really wants in the future. And so you've started to make it all possible.

CHAPTER 7

When your fire burns

Self-care will reignite your power and connect you with the cosmic body.

There's a fire inside of you. It's a light that burns and burns, and it keeps you safe. It burns away all that you don't need, and it's hot enough to burn away everything that's hurt you.

Your inner fire keeps you safe in the way that your *fear* has always wanted to keep you safe. But fear cannot keep you safe because it lies. It can't help it; it's biased. Fear is based only on the worst things that have happened to you – it has no comprehension of all the amazing things that are possible. Fear cannot imagine there's anything that you don't need to be afraid of. It only knows the worst of life.

But the fire inside of you knows more. It knows that fear is a valuable friend – someone you can learn from and who knows secrets that are worth listening to. But it also knows that fear is never, ever a good leader. Your fire welcomes fear to help it avoid steering you into the worst possible situations, but it knows that fear is often dishonest or wrong and that it wants you to avoid anything that's uncertain or mysterious.

And your fire knows that brilliant possibilities lie in the unknown.

But sometimes, our trauma puts out our inner fire. We're flooded with emotion and pain – and yes, fear. We're overloaded. Overwhelmed. So we turn away from the fire and it cools and flickers out.

Now it's time to care for that flame. To reconnect with the power you've always had and burn away the obstacles that life's thrown in your way. Because this isn't a destructive fire – it's the fire of your inner healing, your inner strength, and your true power.

Taking care of your self

Self-care is integral to raising your vibration; but remember, it involves taking care of your mind, body, and spirit, or, as we've illustrated in this book, our bodies. Many of us neglect the work required for the mind to thrive. It's fine to respond to your negative thoughts with positive, empowering ones – turning *I can't do this* into *I've done it before and I can do it again* – but if you have an underlying feeling of sadness, anger or fear, you must reprogram the mind.

You must seek to *transform* your emotions, instead of ignoring them by masking them with positive thoughts that don't fuel a change in your state. You're already doing this by uncovering the deep-rooted beliefs that affect how you feel every day, or in moments of hardship. You *must* address these beliefs.

You must seek to *transform* your emotions, instead of ignoring them by masking them with positive thoughts that don't fuel a change in your state. You're already doing this by uncovering the deep-rooted beliefs that affect how you feel every day, or in moments of hardship. You *must* address these beliefs.

And it's important to add to this by building self-care practices and techniques into your day-to-day life (my first book is packed with ideas for effectively and lovingly caring for yourself). The self-care practices that work for you could be those with which you're already familiar; or they might be things that are currently a bit alien to you, and that you have to try in order to find out if they suit you.

We've already worked with some avenues for creating change, and now I'd like you to take the time to explore nourishing your whole self through simple daily tasks and/or practices such as journaling, meditation, affirmations, Emotional Freedom Technique (EFT), visualization, and breathwork. Don't worry, you don't need to do all of those things – the point is to figure out what works for you and then make it a regular part of your life.

No matter what's in front of us, if the lens we're using to perceive it is cracked, it will never look and feel as good as it's meant to. Self-care is a simple way to fill the cracks in your lens with gold.

Practice #10: Build a self-care routine

You might be wondering why this practice doesn't appear earlier in the book – after all, as I mentioned in Chapter 3, self-care is essential to healing. We can't heal if we're not taking care of ourselves, and feeling well and centered and nourished.

Nevertheless, the reason I want you to build your self-care routine now, at this late stage in the process, is because good self-care practices that really suit *you* are much easier to establish if you're already pretty clear about what you need and how you're feeling. And the work we've done so far means that you're now ready to be honest about what works for you.

Although there are some fundamental practices that can help everyone, self-care doesn't look the same from one individual to the next. One person might feel supported and refreshed by a bath and a cup of tea, or a massage, while another might need a tough workout and a cold shower to feel that sense of being cleansed and ready for whatever lies ahead.

It's not only that. At the start of this process your understanding of self-care might have been limited to the physical body, but now, having moved through this book, you're in touch with the other six bodies that interweave and interrelate.

You're connected with your wholeness, which means you can build a self-care routine that acts on deeper levels. Subconsciously, you can feel when your subtle bodies are energized and cared for, and when they're not. And you're much more skilled at knowing how to give them what they need. To give *you* what you need.

Self-care matters

First, find a quiet space and get comfortable. Ground yourself by closing your eyes and taking three deep, cleansing breaths, so you can be fully present for this exercise. Now grab your notebook and pen – along with a drink or a snack (or both) if it helps you focus into the moment. And then...

1. Title three pages of your notebook. The first page is 'Daily self-care,' the second is 'Weekly self-care,' and the third is 'Monthly self-care.'
2. Take a bird's-eye view of your average day. Even the busiest among us have at least two or three 10–30 minute slots each day that we usually spend scrolling mindlessly through our phone, or lying in bed wishing the day wouldn't start, or watching Netflix shows that don't make us feel great. (I've nothing against watching TV to unwind, but try to do it in moderation, and out of choice rather than habit.)

At the top of your 'Daily self-care' page, make a note of those slots. They'll become your go-to self-care moments to fill with good stuff.

3. Start your self-care practices research. I don't mean just reading things online – although a bit of that can be helpful – I mean hands-on, experiential research. Make a list of practices you want to try, and then *try them*. See how they feel.

   Decide how long your research period is going to be. I recommend a week, or two weeks if you're really short on spare time. But restrict it, so it doesn't go on forever; you've got to stay purposeful.

   ~ Don't know what EFT is? Hit YouTube and use a guided video to try it out.

   ~ Never done a yoga sun salutation? Again, YouTube is your friend. Search for 'sun salutation video' and learn the sequence. This is a great self-care practice to weave into your daily routine because one sun salute takes less than five minutes, and it stretches out all the major muscle groups.

   ~ Never tried journaling? Write down your thoughts, in whatever order they come to mind, for 10 minutes.

   ~ Never taken a bath with essential oils and candles? Do it. (Seriously.)

- Unsure what breathwork entails? Search on Google for different types of breathing exercises and try them out. You'll come across a variety of techniques to try, from yoga (Pranayama) to more recent practices such as the Wim Hof Method.

Try out any and every self-care practice you've ever been interested in – and some that are completely new to you.

Here are some more ideas: Read five pages of a book; write down eight things you're grateful for; get up and go straight outside for a walk around the block; start your day with a healthy smoothie; write out all your thoughts until your mind feels clear; take a spin class; learn to lift weights; drive out to a forest and walk among the trees; try chanting a powerful mantra (hello again, YouTube); lie on the floor with your legs up against a wall for 10 minutes; moisturize your whole body. Anything, anything, anything. Try it all. This is *your* research.

4. When you try a self-care practice that feels good, and makes you feel calm and whole and steady, write it down. And then return to your notebook. First, note down the *daily* practices with which you're going to fill your self-care slots. Then note the *weekly* practices that will help to add a positive structure to each seven-day period. These will be slightly longer ones – things like a big workout, a walk in a forest, and so on.

Next, consider what you'd like to do *once a month* to give yourself a real boost. You may or may not have included these things in your research. How about... carving out time to spend with a good friend when neither of you is on your way to somewhere else; spending a night somewhere other than your home; visiting family who don't live nearby; seeing a therapist; getting a really good massage; meditating for an entire morning, or taking an entire morning just for yourself.

These are all just ideas. This is *your* self-care routine. Only yours. It needs to work for you, and only you.

And once you have this routine in place you can use it as a way to stay with your healing work. To keep returning to yourself. It doesn't need to look the same as the self-care routine of someone you follow online. And you don't need to post it to your social media pages (unless you want to, which is also fine). It's just yours.

It's time for the light

Let's go back to that inner fire for a minute... When have you felt brightest? And when have you felt the most darkness? Have you ever felt that incredible brightness follows a time of deep, impenetrable darkness?

There was a woman called Jeanette (I've changed her name to protect her identity) who had a nice enough life, and got on with her straightforward job without any complaints. She wasn't very happy, but she wasn't at all unhappy either. Everything was just fine.

Until the day everything changed. On her walk home along the River Thames in London one evening, she cut through Borough Market to get to her bus stop. The outdoor food market was full of people having after-work drinks and sitting at tables set outside the restaurants that lined the narrow streets. Jeannette walked through the market, down a little alleyway, and out onto the main road.

Suddenly, she heard screams. People ran toward her, as fast as they could, away from something. And then she saw a man with a knife. He was waving it frantically and lunging toward people. Some people lay on the ground, apparently motionless.

Jeanette froze. She couldn't move. People screamed at her to 'Go!' but everyone was more focused on getting themselves out of the way, pushing past her and rushing for cover. The air was thick with panic. Then she saw policemen, who appeared as if from nowhere.

They were armed, and shouting; and then other policemen ran toward her, holding out their arms and pushing people.

Jeanette ran.

She ran as fast as she could. Faster than she'd ever run in her life. Other people were throwing themselves into restaurants and shops – getting inside, under cover – but she didn't. She just ran. And she kept running. She says she's not sure how long she ran for, but judging by where she was when she stopped, it must've been an hour or more. Her fear propelled her onward, and she never felt tired or out of breath. In fact, she never fully registered why she was running. She just ran. Her flight response was in full control of her body, and her conscious mind had taken a back seat.

When she made it back to her home, Jeanette turned on her computer and read the news. There'd been a terrorist attack on London Bridge and in Borough Market. She felt detached, as if she were reading about an incident on the other side of the world.

But she'd been there. She wasn't ready to acknowledge it, but she'd lived through it, and she'd run for her life.

Over the next few weeks, the reality of this experience began to sink in. Jeanette's state of shock had protected her from the moment and switched off her usual thought processes. Act now, think later – that's what fear like this tells us to do. And we need that because it can save our life.

But then, at some point, we have to start thinking again. And as Jeanette started to think, she found it almost impossible to process what'd happened. People had been dying right in front of her, and she'd stood there, frozen. And then she'd run. Men had been trying to kill everyone they could reach. If they'd reached *her* – if she'd stayed frozen for just a few seconds longer – they could have killed her.

Why hadn't she died? Why had those other people died? Why had these men wanted to kill everyone in such a violent and meaningless way? People they didn't know; people who had families, who were innocent, and were just doing what they did on an evening after work.

As Jeanette sank into darkness, her inner fire went out. She was lost, and everything was black. She thought, repeatedly, that she'd die. She said she didn't want to die, but she didn't know how she could carry on living. Nothing made sense anymore. But somehow, she did keep going.

One of the few good things about Jeanette's experience was that it was so public, and so clearly traumatic, that everyone knew about it. Everyone understood how bad she must have felt, and they all wanted to help. She didn't have to keep her fear a secret, in the way that many people do when they go through a more private traumatic event. She could ask for support; and after a while, she did ask. She got therapy, talked to friends, asked people to go with her when she went out, so she'd feel less afraid.

Six months after the attack, Jeanette returned to the area of London where it'd happened. She'd avoided that place, even though the quickest route to and from work was right through it. But she went back and stood exactly where she'd stood that evening, frozen. She closed her eyes and focused inward. She allowed the memories to flood back: the feelings, the shock, the utter confusion and the primal, animal fear.

She took a deep breath. And when she opened her eyes, she felt a light come back on. Her flame began to burn again.

Today, Jeanette's doing something new – she left her perfectly fine job, got a loan, and started university, where she's studying psychology and trauma therapy. She's going to become a therapist because she wants to help people come to terms with unimaginable experiences. She went through the darkest time of her life, but now, she says, she's never felt brighter or stronger.

I'm sure you're reading this book because, at some point, you've been in the dark. Or you're in the dark right now. It's time for the light. You've spent enough time in fear. And it starts with your inner fire. Make friends with it, protect it, listen to it, and let it burn.

Practice #11: Care for your fire with candle gazing

This practice is based on an ancient meditative practice called trataka, or 'candle gazing.' It sort of does what it says on the tin – you gaze at a candle. But I've taken the benefits of this practice and expanded them into a fuller one that involves visualization and journaling, too.

The benefits of candle gazing, as described in the book *Sure Ways to Self-Realization*,[29] and backed up in a cognitive study published by the *International Journal of Yoga*,[30] include the following:

---

29 Swami Satyananda Saraswati (2008), *Sure Ways to Self-Realization*. Yoga Publications Trust.

30 Talwadkar, S., et al. (2014), 'Effect of trataka on cognitive functions in the elderly': www.ijoy.org.in/text.asp?2014/7/2/96/133872 [Accessed January 15, 2020]

No matter what's in front of us,
if the lens we're using to perceive
it is cracked, it will never look
and feel as good as it's meant to.
Self-care is a simple way to fill the
cracks in your lens with gold.

- Strengthened eye muscles and improved focus – not only the physical focus of the eyes, but also our ability to concentrate.
- A relaxed mind and body; it's also been found to improve sleep quality.
- A calmed nervous system and a reduction in anxiety.
- Improved mental clarity, making way for a clearer sense of self and purpose.

And when candle gazing is combined with the visualization and journaling practice we'll do here, you will:

- Feel connected to your inner fire – your motivation, your protection, your burning energy. You'll use that energy to burn away fear and insecurity, arriving at a steady sense of who you are and how you want to live in the world from this moment onward.
- Be able to reconnect with your fire whenever it feels dull or weak, and remind yourself of why you're dedicated to this inner healing work.

Fire it up

You'll need a pen and your notebook, open at a blank page; a candle, secure in a candlestick holder (a simple tealight will also do fine); and matches or a lighter. And a quiet, private room that can be darkened; for this reason, the practice is best done in the evening, after sunset, or very early in the morning, before sunrise.

1. Make the room dark. Switch off the lights and any screens that are illuminated. Close the curtains/blinds and the door.

2. Sit on a chair, and place the candle on a table in front of you, so it's more or less at eye level. Light the candle.

3. Blink rapidly for a few seconds and shake your head to release tension in the neck. Then focus your gaze on the candle flame. Allow everything else in the room to disappear. You're completely focused on the flame, and only the flame.

   Do not blink. Keep your gaze on the flame for as long as you possibly can without blinking. Your eyes will start to water. Stay focused. Then, when you really can't keep your eyes open and on the flame any longer, close them.

4. Notice the colors and shapes you see behind your eyelids. Impressions from the flame. Shifting shapes and images. Brightness, contrasting with the dark.

5. Then, as that brightness shifts and changes, imagine that it's becoming an image of the flame within you. Your flame. Your fire. In the darkness behind your eyelids you see your fire burning – a reflection of the light and strength inside of you.

   It gets stronger, and brighter. Maybe the flame fills your vision completely, and then it fills your mind completely. And then it fills your body completely. It feels like warmth, and strength, and happiness. It feels like potential. And as it burns, it burns away fear. It burns away the limiting beliefs that have held you back for such a long time. It burns away everything that stops you from stepping into who you truly are.

   You know this flame is your own. It's always been there, even when the darkness around you has been too thick for you to see it. It will always be there.

6. Rub the palms of your hands together to generate some heat. Place the palms over your eyes and gently blink into your hands; let the light from the candle filter through your fingers. Then move your hands away, turn on a lamp or ceiling light, and blow out the candle.

7. On the blank page of your notebook, write down whatever thoughts come into your head. It doesn't matter what they are, or if they seem to be irrelevant. Let them out. Put them down. Fill one page. You could write in free-form, stream-of-consciousness style, or simply make quick bullet points to lay out your thoughts.

8. Finally, take one deep breath. Fill your lungs with oxygen, and then breathe it all out.

CHAPTER 8

You are free

Nirvana is freedom. It's not a place, but a state of the self – and an expression of being whole. Of healing.

Here are some things that freedom might feel like to you:

- Lightness.
- Openness – as if you've been hunched over and closed inward and now you're expansive and huge and ready to welcome everything.
- A sense of being complete and whole.
- Feeling connected to everything around you, as if you really are the wave that knows it's a part of the ocean and always will be.
- Being a city house cat that's finally moved into the countryside and gets to roam through fields and forests. You're a bit unsure because this is all so new, but you've never felt more like a *cat*.

- Cycling down a long, empty, smooth-surfaced road on the side of a hill that's not so steep it's scary, but just steep enough that you go joyfully fast and the wind blows away the cobwebs.
- Making a decision that feels completely right.
- Being confident that the bad things that happened in your past cannot continue to hurt you indefinitely.
- Excitement for the future.
- Going out without worrying about what time you have to head home.
- Not watching the clock.
- Not worrying about what other people think of you.
- Not expecting the worst.
- Knowing that all kinds of good things are going to happen.
- Knowing that even when you experience difficult times again, you have everything you need to get through them.
- Not feeling scared (*all* the time). You'll still feel scared sometimes; you might even feel scared of freedom sometimes. It's all good.
- Knowing you can be free in every moment.

This is the new high

You've taken charge of your inner healing. You're your own healer. I call you that now because you really are. I mean, you always have been, but now you know how to use all the wisdom within you. You're doing it. The progress you've made has nothing to do with a guru or an outside healing force: you've simply gained some tools that allow you to connect with the guide inside you. You've opened up a new conversation with yourself by connecting with your inner light. It's in this place that your inner fire and wisdom open the door to transmutation.

And, as I mentioned many pages ago, taking charge of your healing in this way is one of the most powerful acts of self-love you can choose. By reading this book and working through the practices within it, you've told yourself that you're worthy of change. You've sent a strong message to your inner world that you're ready to raise your vibration and live higher. Nothing gets to keep you down anymore.

You're returning to equilibrium. You might not feel as if you're quite there yet, and that's natural. This is a journey, after all, and there's no clear end. We'll be healing and hurting and healing again for the rest of our lives.

But what you're doing, every time you refocus on your journey, is lifting yourself into a higher vibrational state. Creating possibilities for yourself, and radiating out powerful energy that will be returned to you. Repeating that message that you're worthy of feeling better, worthy of change, and that you ultimately deserve to feel free.

Healing isn't only about healing – it's about your entire life. If you're seeking success and have goals to achieve, it's vital to focus your energy on your inner self. Recovering from your emotional wounds is an important step if you want to change your life in a big way.

So, healing isn't just for spiritual types, or 'hippies,' or whatever you want to call them. Healing is necessary for anyone who wants change. I've said it before – there's no tricking the Universe. If you're vibrating low because of emotional pain, no amount of external effort will lift your vibration for very long. You've got to start within, and enable yourself to put out the positive energy that you wish to receive back.

Practice #12: Float into it

An important part of experiencing freedom is knowing that you're a part of the fabric of the Universe. Not just knowing this with your brain, but feeling it, embodying it, knowing it with every cell, every

Healing isn't only about healing – it's about your entire life. If you're seeking success and have goals to achieve, it's vital to focus your energy on your inner self. Recovering from your emotional wounds is an important step if you want to change your life in a big way.

subtle energy flow, every part of you. Knowing that you're not the wave, you're the ocean.

As with all of the progress you've made so far, and will make in the future, this isn't a one-time thing. You won't experience this kind of liberating oneness *once*, and then be certain of it for the rest of your life. It will come and go. You're human, and your existence isn't perpetually moving in one direction in a clean and simple manner. It's complex, and your journey has twists and turns. Healing is messy.

Freedom isn't always easy to access. But it gets easier to access if you practice it; if you actively engage in a conscious process of freeing yourself. Which is exactly what this exercise is.

Becoming

Get settled. As always, you'll need to be in a quiet and comfortable place, free from disturbances. Take your time to make the adjustments you need to make: closing doors, putting on (or taking off) clothing to make sure you're a comfortable temperature. Anything you need to do.

1. **Find your seated posture. If you feel comfortable sitting upright without support for your back, great; but if not, feel free to sit on a chair that supports your spine, or sit on the floor with your**

back against a wall. The goal isn't to adopt a formal meditation posture, but to feel steady and comfortable, and able to focus on your practice without being distracted by an aching back, hips, or shoulders.

2. Close your eyes and take a few deep, full breaths. Breathe in through the nose and out through the mouth. The out breath could be gentle, or you could turn it into a powerful, loud sigh – whatever helps you to feel relaxed, to arrive in the present moment, and to let go of the rest of the day up to this point. Then allow the breath to settle into a natural rhythm.

3. Notice the body. The parts of the body that are supported by the ground, the floor, or the furniture beneath you. The parts of the body that feel warmer or cooler than others.

   Notice the length of the spine – from the very bottom, right up to the top.

   Notice the weight of the eyelids.

   Allow yourself to be here, and only here. Because there's nowhere else to be. Nothing else to do.

4. Now, bring the awareness to the center of the chest. We're noticing this area – the heart and the space around it – because this freedom practice isn't just about the mind. We're going to use the mind to

do it, but it's working on every aspect of your being. It's a practice of the heart as much as a practice of the mind.

So, notice the heart. Notice the chest. As you breathe, allow the chest to expand. The shoulders broaden slightly. The chest opens. The heart opens. The space that grows there is a space of connection, and you feel your constant, unshakable connection with a greater whole.

Say the following statement, or affirmation, out loud, or silently in your mind: *With an open heart, I'm connected with oneness.*

5. Allow this openness and expansion in the chest to remain – without force – as you begin to visualize yourself standing on a beach.

   Really take the time to put yourself there. Notice the sand or pebbles beneath your feet; the textures against your bare skin. See the color of the sky and the ocean out ahead of you. You can smell the salt on the air. Feel the gentle breeze brushing against you. You can hear the waves, softly lapping at the shore.

   You stand at the edge of the ocean. Looking out.

6. And then, when you feel present in this moment at the edge of the ocean, dip a toe into the water. You lift your leg – feeling the muscles working, the extension of your toes toward the ocean. Then you feel the coolness enveloping you as your toe touches the water.

And you notice that as soon as you come into contact with the ocean, you become water. That toe becomes water; it's still you, and yet it's water. You move your foot further into the ocean and as you do so, your whole foot becomes water.

7. When you pull your foot out, it's as it was before: your foot. Skin, bone, muscle.

   Curiously, you decide to go further – because you feel the power of becoming one with the water. You feel the strength of being not only *you*, but also something bigger.

8. You step into the ocean with both feet. Gradually, you go further out and as each part of your body is submerged, it becomes water. Until you are water – all of you. You're a part of this expansive blue, and it feels *good*.

   You lie on your back with your water body, feeling perfectly supported and held by the ocean. You float on your back, gazing up from this altered state, and you're no longer held captive by doubt, uncertainty, or insecurity, or fear.

   Because you're not alone. Not ever. You're supposed to be here. You're a part of this. You always have been, and you always will be.

9. Take your time here. There's no rush.

And then, when you feel ready, gently make your way back to the shore. Perhaps you swim, or simply move there effortlessly.

You stand up and your body resumes its usual form.

You take a few easy breaths, and look out at the ocean again. And a gentle smile spreads across your face because you're not trapped in any perceived or prescribed version of yourself, or of who anyone thinks you're supposed to be.

With that smile, you say again: *With an open heart, I'm connected with oneness.*

10. Finally, in your own time, bring your awareness back to your breath. Take in three deep, slow breaths through your nose and slowly let them out through your mouth.

    And when you're ready, gently and slowly open your eyes.

A truth: You won't feel good all the time

Inner freedom doesn't mean being happy all the time. It doesn't mean that on every occasion you step outside the house you'll stride confidently with a big grin on your face (although I hope you do that often).

This might not sound like the most uplifting way to connect you with your inner freedom; however, it's an incredibly important thing to understand because if you don't, somewhere down the line you might think that you're doing something wrong.

This really genuine kind of freedom is actually about acceptance, and a calm sense of knowing. You're free because you're not dreading the moment when something difficult happens. You're free because you know that whatever comes your way, you'll be able to accept it and work through it. You're free because you welcome the full range of emotions that are part of being a living, breathing, feeling human.

And your ultimate strength is knowing that you can return to equilibrium; that your true, peaceful Self is always there, no matter how much clutter and outside stuff is muddling how you interpret things in any given moment. The surface might be choppy and hard to handle, but the water beneath is always still. You're capable of looking beneath the surface and seeing that the stillness is always there.

Free yourself when feeling stuck

You're in the seventh body now. Working into it, meditating through it with each word you read. But don't forget that all of the bodies are interconnected, all of the time. Whenever you feel trapped and disconnected from any sense of freedom, go back. Go to the physical body and move it. Run like a wild child, swim in a river, jump up and down, stretch, work out, do yoga. Freedom in the physical body is one of the quickest ways to feel freedom on a deeper lever when you're feeling stuck.

Everything we've done in these pages has been leading to freedom. Because at the end of it all, that's what self-healing is – shedding the weight of the past, letting go, and being liberated. But again, this journey isn't linear.

Sometimes we need to do something to remind ourselves what this freedom feels like for a few seconds or minutes or hours, so we don't forget what we're doing all of this for. So here are a few things you can do when you're feeling stuck to quickly feel free:

- Take off all your clothes. Not appropriate in all situations, I know... but it works. Even better if you can do it outside. You could even take off all your clothes and safely jump into a cold river or the sea (provided you can swim).

Whenever you feel disconnected from any sense of freedom, go to the physical body and move it. Run like a wild child, swim in a river, jump up and down, work out, do yoga. Freedom in the physical body is a quick way to feel freedom on a deeper level.

- Laugh. Ideally with someone else, but you can laugh on your own, too. It always helps if there's something funny to laugh at, but have you ever tried laughing at... nothing? You can. The ridiculousness of it makes you laugh even more. Or you could try 'laughter yoga.'[31]
- Tell someone something really honest – be real but don't be rude.
- Take a day off in the middle of the week and spend every minute of it outside. From sunrise to sunset.
- Meditate.
- Switch up your schedule. Bump the stressful thing you're procrastinating over, and do something else.
- Tell someone that you're finding something hard and ask for their help.
- Dance. But *really* dance. Forget self-consciousness and put on some music and move in whatever weird way you feel like moving.

31 Laughter Yoga University, 'What is Laugher Yoga & how can it help you?': https://laughteryoga.org/laughter-yoga/about-laughter-yoga [Accessed January 8, 2021]

- Go somewhere and do an activity completely on your own.
- Walk down the stairs backward (be careful, obviously).
- Get up early and go for a walk while everyone else in the house/town is still asleep.
- Start learning something you've always wanted to learn.

Practice #13: Walk in freedom

It feels a bit strange to write down this practice – it's the last one, which means this process we've been working through together is coming to an end. But not exactly...

Although you'll reach the end of this book, your journey is really just beginning. You're in a very exciting place – ready to go on and take everything you've learnt into your life. Some of the practices we've done might stay with you as your journey ebbs and flows – use them whenever you need to. Although we talk about it as a journey, this process is not a linear one. It's not a matter of getting from A to B and then you're done. It's a lifelong process of learning, growing, changing, and relearning.

And there will be setbacks; everyone has setbacks. Everyone has days when they feel like they've completely lost track of where they're meant to be and have fallen back into old habits and patterns and need to start again from scratch.

Off days are fine. Even off weeks, or months, or years. What's important is that you get back in touch with your capacity to heal yourself. Remember that *you* are your own healer, and you've all the tools you need. So *use* them.

I have off days. I feel stuck sometimes, and I have a sense that all the good work I've done, and the steps I've put in place, have come undone. Something triggers me in a strong way and I drop right back into a state of fear. But then I remember that I have the tools. All of the practices I've shared with you in this book are useful for *me*, too.

So, even though we're getting into our last practice now, we're still journeying together. And hey, I'm on Instagram, in case you hadn't heard...

Time to get out there

This exercise is a walk. But not just any walk – it's a walk in your new sense of freedom.

1. Head outside. If it's possible, get out into nature – a forest, fields, near a river, the ocean. But if it's not, a city walk is equally abundant with opportunities to enjoy your freedom.

2. Walk. Loosen up your body. Hold your head high. Even smile if you want to. Take big, relaxed, and confident steps. Not in a hurry, but not dawdling. Feel freedom in every step.

3. As you walk, notice what's around you. Take it all in. Plants, trees, buildings, people, animals, vehicles, the weather, the sky, clouds, sunshine, all of it.

4. And notice what's within you. For the duration of this practice, know that you're free. Nothing that has hurt you in the past is here, holding you back. You're striding peacefully and happily along without any worries or fears.

   You're practicing the subversive art of walking in the world with a deep sense of freedom. You know that you're free. (Don't worry if, generally speaking, you're not really there yet. You don't have to feel 'healed.' Just let yourself be free while you're doing this walk.)

5. Keep going. *Enjoy* it. Let it be one of the best experiences of your life so far, this simple, uncomplicated walk.

6. Walk until you're ready to stop. And when you do stop and go home or back to work or wherever you're going, give yourself a few minutes to adjust. Instead of jumping straight into the thing you're doing next, stand or sit still. Breathe deeply. And smile.

Why is this the final practice in the book? Because it's time to show up in the world as you. No more hiding. There's no one else like you, and your uniqueness is needed. Honestly, it is.

How will you know if your efforts are working?

There's no single answer to this question because it's personal; and one individual's signs of healing could change over time, too. But in general, all of the below are strong indicators that the work you're doing is truly having an important positive impact:

- Even when you do feel triggered (and it will still happen), you're able to return to a state of calmness and steadiness more quickly than before, and are less likely to spiral into days, weeks, or months of a triggered state.

Off days are fine. Even off weeks, or months, or years. What's important is that you get back in touch with your capacity to heal yourself. Remember that *you* are your own healer, and you have all the tools you need. So *use* them.

- You feel generally stronger and more confident, and notice that your insecurity has subsided; you recognize your own power to change your situation.
- You can more easily predict when you're going to be triggered by a situation or an interaction, and can prepare yourself for it.
- You feel less ashamed of your pain, and more comfortable about expressing yourself; you have more confidence that other people will listen to you, and respect you.
- That feeling of being stuck in one place, with no hope of ever moving forward, has lessened – you more frequently feel that you can move on and build a happier and more fulfilling life.
- Your visualizations or fantasies about the future are filled with hope instead of disaster.

Freedom for me...

Freedom feels different to different people. For me, the most telling experience of feeling completely liberated on my self-healing journey came when I realized that I'd no longer be shown or told what my life should look like.

Comparison and judgment were regular features of my childhood, and failures seemed to be bolder than successes. Which made me feel that I wasn't good enough. Now, although I accept that I can be and do better (as growth is constant and essential), I also balance this with acceptance of who I am (self-love).

The fear of judgment is real. Even when I accepted my calling to help others, I had to face the social awkwardness of being judged by my peers for leaving a respectful, steady corporate job, a thriving industry, and a luxurious lifestyle to follow a higher purpose. In fact, when I told the manager of my last corporate job I was leaving to pursue something greater, he told me I'd struggle to go from a great salary to nothing. He refused to believe that *I* believed in my own dreams, and he said that he wouldn't be surprised if, after leaving that job, I went through depression and killed myself.

But it wasn't *his* words that struck me the deepest. It was those of my closest friends and family members who told my other loved ones that I'd become a bum. A nobody without money, status, or stability who was chasing unrealistic dreams.

After the release and reach of my first book – which I'm extremely grateful for – I could have rebuilt my identity and rubbed it in their faces. But I felt no animosity toward them; in fact, I celebrated with some of them. If I had felt any hostility toward them, it would have meant they still had control over me – and that my self-worth was still dependent on their opinions of me. But thankfully, I've done the work and I live for me, even if that means helping others with no expectation of getting anything in return.

Today when people ask me what I do, I'm comfortable saying, 'I just try to help people,' while reminding myself that I'm not defined by titles and labels. I've nothing to prove, so I don't try to sell myself to others.

I know the people who ask me that question sometimes hold preconceived ideas, and I'll never be able to stop them from judging me. But my inner response is, *who cares?* Not as a form of apathy, but as acceptance, and a reminder that it doesn't matter to me what other people think. I chose something meaningful, and ultimately, their perception of me is a reflection of them– they see me through their past conditioning and trauma. However, I've chosen to live as my true Self – and I couldn't feel freer.

I'm living my life on my own terms. I no longer fall victim to opinions and judgment. Rarely do these people live rent-free in my mind. When I meet someone new I'm not worried about what they'll think of me, because I *know* what I think of myself, and I *know* that other people's judgments don't change who I am. Peace of mind is the real luxury, and true freedom, and I have it in abundance.

And freedom for you?

It's all to come. Life is wide open.

If there's one more thing I'd like to ask you to do, it's to trust. Trust that you can feel free; that you will. And when it happens, and you're in that moment and feeling the lightness and openness and peace, trust that it's real and that you deserve it.

Your pain isn't talking. Fear isn't taking the lead. *You* are.

Closing thoughts

As I write this book, we're all going through something that none of us has ever been through before. The coronavirus pandemic has changed the whole planet, and all of our lives, in just a few months. And so, inevitably, I'm imagining how this time will impact us in the future. Will it add new layers of trauma to many of our lives? How will the uncertainty, and the undercurrent of instability running through all of our choices and actions, affect how we come to see the world?

I've no doubt that living through such a challenging time has reignited memories of past trauma for some. Even those of us who were pretty lucky, and who weren't out there providing medical care or witnessing tragedies every day, and who were on lockdown in not-too-tiny homes with people we were happy to be locked in with... even we will almost definitely carry new trauma with us as a result.

Right now, as I write, we're in crisis mode. We're dealing with it. We're getting through the days and doing what we have to do to adapt and make our lives work in this pared-down world. Getting used to standing on taped lines on shop floors, and crossing the street to avoid being too close to other people.

Getting used to the reality that we can't just go and visit our parents, or siblings, or friends – and that getting together with people now happens on Zoom. In some parts of the world, people are adjusting to having to fill in a form every time they want to leave the house. And a vast number of us are trying to manage life-changing loss of work.

We're dealing with it. And later on, we'll hit a point when we have to deal with it in a different way, and process the fear that this experience might have filled us with.

Wherever you are, my heart goes out to you. I hope that you and your loved ones are as safe and well as you can be.

But there's also a part of me that already sees the light that will come from this. Our society has been forced to change, and we've been forced to reflect, and whatever happens, the impact of this will be lasting. We're not going to go back to the way we were before; at least not exactly.

And it's interesting to be on lockdown in this unprecedented situation and to be writing a book about trauma. To be calling friends and hearing their anxiety and fear, seeing their tears on video chat... and then to hang up and write about healing practices, and reconnecting with ourselves fully after trauma, and freedom.

To be on lockdown while writing about inner freedom – is there irony in that? Or is there some kind of fateful purpose? It feels somehow that this book *had* to be written during a strange and uncertain time. It's enabled me to reconnect with some of the complicated feelings I'd left behind, and I hope that's reflected in the form of empathy and understanding in these pages.

I hope this book can help you as you move on with life. Writing it has definitely helped me to accept where I'm at right now, and to appreciate the people who are here with me.

I hope you take strength and positivity from these pages. And confidence. I hope you feel more confident that you can, and are, recovering. Heal. Feel your own power. I completely believe that you can, and are, healing.

I won't count the number of times I've said that this is *your* journey and *your* healing work. To be done on nobody else's schedule. But what I haven't said – and it's something that I also know to be true – is that although this journey is profoundly personal, it also benefits everyone. The more people who accept themselves, and know how to care for themselves and heal from challenges and trauma, the better. Because each one of those people, including you, will go out into the world and radiate more love, kindness, hope, and positive innovation.

People who accept themselves can accept others. And that can change the world.

Thank you for being here. I truly appreciate your commitment to these pages.

Wishing you nothing but the best,

Afterword
A dedication

There's only one person I can dedicate this book to: My heart, my queen, my love, my wife, Kaushal.

You've been on a tremendous journey. I mean, wow. Witnessing your growth and how much you've achieved since I met you has been one of the highlights of my life. I couldn't be prouder – not only as your husband, but also as someone who loves to see people do the unthinkable; when these are the people you love dearly, though, it means so much more. You've been an inspiration.

With everything you've achieved in your career, and with the vast platform you've built, you've had your fair share of struggles. I know that, like all humans, you're prone to making mistakes, but from the day I met you, I can honestly say you've been one of the most sincere and kindest souls I know.

Your goal wasn't to be rich and famous. You weren't concerned about being adored by many; you simply wanted to share what you love. And with that attitude in mind, you were able to connect with the hearts of millions, which changed your life forever. You've managed to manifest a life filled with blessings and opportunities that one could only dream of – something I know you're truly grateful for.

Nevertheless, along with the exposure has come heartache. Seeing you get bullied and hurt hasn't been easy for me. Especially as I know the capacity of your heart and the innocence that gleams from you. Your mental health journey has been painful to witness. I admit that at times, I've felt hopeless and powerless, especially when you refused to speak to me about it. In these moments, my self-image shattered as I fed myself stories about how my help wasn't good enough for you, and that maybe it was somehow my fault that you didn't feel confident enough to speak to me.

Admittedly, I even pondered on the possibility that our love wasn't as strong as I imagined it to be – given that you couldn't pour your heart out to me. This is what the ego does – it skews our perception, makes us victims, and distorts the truth.

I know that to the world I'm often viewed as a guy with answers, a coach, a guide, or a change worker, but to you, I'm a husband...

and that's what I kept reminding myself and showing up as. While you were struggling, I tried to keep that boundary in place and be there for you, but deep down, I wanted to help you on your inward journey so you could be who you are deep down – the joyful girl who's unbounded by love.

Like every couple, we have disagreements, and during that period, we probably experienced more than our average. Throughout our journey, our wounds have gotten the better of us, and we've often allowed the waves of our trauma to drown each other out. But we've never given up on each other. We've continued to turn up – ready to resolve and evolve. This is why our journey is so special.

While I wished I could be the one to help you, when I recommended that you attend therapy, I knew it was the right thing to do. I also know how frightening the idea was for you. You were afraid of confronting the parts of you that you'd hidden for so long – you weren't ready for the revelations that would come to light. I understand how uncomfortable that must have been, as my own healing journey has been filled with discomfort. That's why I'm so proud of you for taking such a courageous step.

At that time, it wasn't an option for you to share with me how you truly felt, and the reasons behind those feelings. You were embarrassed to admit what challenged you on a daily basis, and you didn't want to pass on to me the burden of your troubles. You knew that if you admitted to everything you were feeling, I'd naturally be concerned for your wellbeing – even through your pain, you were looking out for me. Thank you for loving me with every corner of your being.

What you don't know is that the entire experience inspired this whole frame of work. It set me on a path to dig deeper – not only within myself, but also with everything I thought I knew about inner healing. I wanted to find a solution – a simple way to approach the process that would allow each and every one of us to be our own healer; *particularly* when therapy isn't an option, or speaking to someone isn't the easiest thing to do. I had to review, refine, and re-establish my existing methods and thinking to develop this body of text.

It's because of your journey that this book exists. After dedicating endless hours to this project, I can confidently say that together, we've discovered something truly special – dare I say, absolutely transformational.

Dear reader,

The hurt, the heartache, and the hell you've been going through... it won't last forever. You will heal. You will experience new highs. Your life will feel like heaven. There's a greater plan for you.

Acknowledgments

There are so many people I could name individually who've made a difference in my life and to the preparation of this book. Without Jane, my agent at Graham Maw Christie, or my family and friends, none of this would have been possible. I thank you all from the bottom of my heart – not only for your support, but also for simply being there for me and with me; whether it was to converse about everyday topics, share a smile or a laugh, celebrate our wins, or discuss our vision for the future. Sometimes, that's all we need to spark our creativity and drive our productivity – some form of inspiration and joy through the people we surround ourselves with.

It's important that I offer thanks to Hay House, not only for assisting and nurturing me throughout these last few years, but also for welcoming me to their family. While I can't name everyone individually, I'd like to thank a few people in particular. Amy: Although you're no longer at Hay House, you gave me the initial opportunity to become a published author. Jo, both Julies and Leanne: The hard work that you do on behalf of all the authors at Hay House UK never goes unnoticed.

Sian, who's no longer at Hay House, and Hannah: You've both shown a great desire to find opportunities for me to be on public forums so my message can travel further and reach new audiences. Diane: Even if it was 11 p.m., you'd read, reply, and then act on each and every one of my emails with nothing but kindness – you've shown great commitment to your role and it's highly admirable. I'm tremendously grateful to my editor, Debra, and her commitment to the process of refining this book. Reid: You not only oversee all of us authors, but you also encourage us to live to our greatest potential.

And finally, Michelle: Thank you for believing in me and trusting me. You get it – my vision to continue to push my message while being authentic, spreading kindness, and empowering others. During your speech at Hay House's 2018 Summer Soirée, you mentioned that although it's important for the business to make a profit, we have to remember why it's here: to assist people with their healing and to make a difference. It was when you said this that I knew I was home – I could live with purpose.

From the beginning of my journey as an author, you've been actively on hand when I've needed support or advice. You've fought my corner for me, and you've kindly given me this opportunity to release another book – without the pressure of delivering it within an impossible timeframe. You've simply told me to trust my intuition, and for that, I have immense gratitude. You've allowed me to be myself.

I'd like to give a special mention to my friend and talented yoga teacher Isla, who helped me find direction with this book, and was always there as a source of inspiration and information throughout the writing journey. And Dr. Bobby Sura from the Solihull Well Being Clinic, for his invaluable expertise, guidance, and feedback while I was finalizing the book.

Finally, I'm genuinely grateful for all the people, above and beyond social media, who support me and inspire me to keep sharing my perspectives. So many of you invested in my first book, and then requested I write another... and with you in mind, I've written this one.

ABOUT THE AUTHOR

© Camissao

Vex King is the #1 *Sunday Times* bestselling author of *Good Vibes, Good Life*, a social media content creator, and a mind coach. He experienced many challenges when he was growing up: his father died when Vex was just a baby, his family were often homeless, and he grew up in troubled neighborhoods where he regularly experienced violence and racism. Despite this, Vex successfully turned his whole life around and is now leading a revolution for the next generation of spiritual seekers.

As a major voice in the world of personal development, Vex shares deep spiritual knowledge in a way that's easy to understand, with stories from his own life, great inspirational quotes, and practical solutions.

For more inspiration from Vex, follow his popular social media platforms (all @vexking) and sign up to his mailing list at vexking.com

vexking.com

Also available:

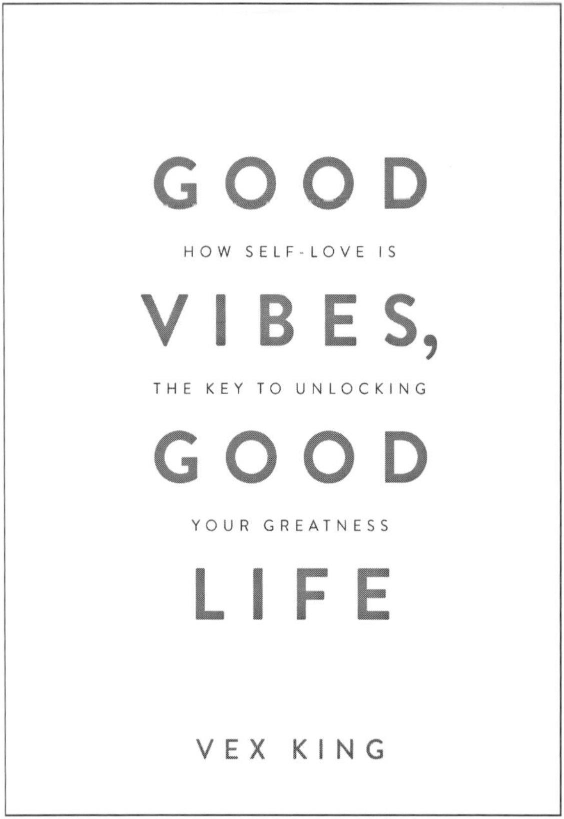

ISBN: 978-93-86832-83-2
Paperback

HAY HOUSE

CONNECT WITH

HAY HOUSE

ONLINE

hayhouse.co.in

@hayhouseindia

@hayhouseindia

@hayhouseindia

Join the conversation about latest products, events, exclusive offers, contests, giveaways and more.

'The gateways to wisdom and knowledge are always open.'

Louise Hay